T0161355

Leveraging Your Leadership Style

John Jackson and Lorraine Bossé-Smith

Jessup University Press

Leveraging Your Leadership Style book and workbook

Copyright © 2015 Jessup University Press
Authors John Jackson & Lorraine Bossé-Smith

ISBN: 978-0-9916111-1-9

What Others are Saying About Leveraging Your Leadership Style:

"John Jackson is a leader of leaders. His insight and foresight challenge me as a leader. And his vision is contagious! If John writes it I'm going to read it."

—**Mark Batterson**, Lead Pastor, National Community Church; Author,
In a Pit with a Lion on a Snowy Day, chasethelion.com

"Lorraine has captured the essence of four key leadership styles in a way that allows everyone from frontline supervisors to CEOs to identify their own leadership characteristics. This book can be a guide to how to more effectively be the right leader at the right time to garner the right results."

—**Jim Canfield**, President and Chief Operating Officer,
Renaissance Executive Forums

"My first thought was, 'Ho hum, another leadership book.' But after a few paragraphs I found this book was different. Looking at leadership through the lens of personality types is refreshing and releases all of us to do more and to do better. John and Lorraine have given us a great tool!"

—**Tim Stevens**, Executive Search Consultant Team Leader,
Vanderbloemen Search Group; Author;
Leadership Thinker on LeadingSmart.com;
and former Pastor at Granger Community Church

"Relationship is far more than just a nice word or idea for Lorraine; it is a way of life. She is one of the most intentional and effective people I know when it comes to developing successful relationships.

Every good leader I know is also good at developing healthy relationships. Lorraine is one of those good leaders. She is the kind of leader people want to follow because of who she is…not simply because of the position she happens to hold.

Although I know she has a wall full of framed certificates to vouch for her professional training in her field, she also clearly has an uncanny intuition when it comes to assessing and understanding people. I believe this something extra comes through loud and clear in this book. Like Lorraine, all of us are unique, and we all lead in some sphere whether it be large or small. The effectiveness of our leadership can only be maximized when we know our God-given style and understand how to leverage it.

For her, this book is not just about a useful theory; it's a parable of her passion for equipping you, me, and others to leverage our leadership style."

—**Gary D. Foster**, Consultant

"My father often reminded me, 'Son,' 'no matter whm you are with or where you are, there is always someone looking up to you for leadership.' This book is for everyone because everyone reading this book has someone following them, believe it nor not. Someone today looked up to you for leadership—intentionally or unintentionally. Was your influence a positive one? You are influencing someone with every verbal and non-verbal communication you send. John and Lorraine will masterfully help you to uncover your leadership potential and style."

—**Dr. Cornell Haan**, National Facilitator for the Mission America Coalition, Co-founder, the Presidential Prayer Team, President, Kingdom Connections

"I was recently interviewed and asked the question, 'What's the number one thing you have learned in ten years of launching the Bayside Family of Churches movement?' I responded, 'That's easy—the solution to everything is the right leader.' John Jackson lives to add value to leaders. I constantly bring him in to evaluate our organization, and mentor our leaders, and his new book, *Leveraging Your Leadership Style* will be in the hands of the staff at all of our churches the minute it comes off the presses."

—**Ray W. Johnston**, Sr. Pastor, Bayside Church, Granite Bay

"I admit it. I'm unique. It impacts who I am and how I interact with others. One of the areas in my life where that's most evident is in my leadership. Leveraging Your Leadership challenges us to consider how our personalities impact how we lead. (That includes leading unique guys like me.)"

—**Tony Morgan**, Pastor, Author, and Consultant

"While I've always believed that leaders are made, not born, I never had a good recipe. You've given me one that's crystal clear with lots of specifics. Anyone who wants to become a leader or fill their company's leadership pipeline should read this book."

—**Laurence Haughton**, Author of the bestseller *It's Not the Big that Eat the Small... It's the FAST that Eat the Slow: How to Use Speed as a Competitive Tool in Business* and *It's Not What You Say... It's What You Do: How Following Through at Every Level Can Make or Break Your Company.*

DISCOVER YOUR LEADERSHIP STYLE!

"Leadership is influence, and no matter what your title or position, you have the opportunity to lead. Since leadership is a matter of motivating, encouraging, and guiding people to a destination together, why not leverage your unique style and influence the people in your life?

"This is not your typical leadership book. *Leveraging Your Leadership Style* takes the guesswork out of the equation and offers concrete solutions to obtain greater results and success.

"The substance of leadership is critical, but style affects how that substance is delivered and perceived. This book will provide you with valuable insights into your own preferred style: What is it and how it can be improved. You'll learn to both understand and appreciate the difference in those you lead."

Mark Sanborn, CSP, CPAE
Author of the bestseller, *The Fred Factor*

"Want to awaken the leader within? Ready to increase your influence and be the leader you were intended to be? Seize the opportunity to transform your leadership with this fast, dynamic, yet informative book that helps you maximize your strengths and become more effective in whatever you do.

"John Jackson is a strategic thinker. He's a visionary. John believes in partnerships and alliances, and he loves working with others. He's not been afraid to ask others to take the journey with him. The result? Thousands are taking that journey today that weren't just a half decade ago."

John Maxwell
Best-Selling Author & America's Leadership Expert

To all the leaders we've known that have inspired us: ordinary everyday folks who used their personal styles for extraordinary influence in the lives of their families, friends, and team members.

We also want to recognize the greatest leader either of us have ever known: Jesus.

CONTENTS

Acknowledgments

I want to thank Lorraine for her insight and energy, which often fueled this project just when it needed it! I also want to thank the various church, ministry, and marketplace teams I have been able to serve with. It always takes a team to win! I also want to acknowledge the wonderful leaders who I've had the privilege to serve with over the years…I'm so thankful they were not "cookie-cutters"…each one a unique individual who led with style.

Finally, my children and their spouses: Jennifer and Derek, Dena and Cheyne, Rachel and Zach, Joshua, and Harrison are always an inspiration. My wife Pamela is my soul mate, my best friend, my protector, and the love of my life…thanks for all you do and who you are, sweetheart.

—**Dr. John Jackson**

I thank God for bringing Dr. John Jackson into my life. I've had the pleasure of working on several projects with him. How exciting to have our books translated in several foreign languages and now have a second edition of *Leveraging Your Leadership Style!* John lives out godly leadership and shares his gifts with us all.

Many years ago, a man presented a training program that inspired and motivated me to be my best. He instilled in me the knowledge that I, too, was a leader, no matter my role. That man was Mark Sanborn, who has become one of the greatest speakers and leadership experts of our times. I thank him for his messages, mentorship, and most of all, his friendship.

I have been fortunate to work for, alongside, and with some other great leaders. They impacted me in a powerful and positive way, helping me become the person I am today. I have also encountered some horrible bosses who didn't understand the meaning of leadership, but I thank God for those lessons, too. I knew who I didn't want to be.

I have been blessed with friends who support, encourage, and pray for me. My best friend and husband, Steve, is a Highliner (if you don't know what that is, you must read his book, *Lessons from the Sea*) who challenges me to always take the path less traveled and to make my mark in the world. When the journey gets tough, he is always there, reminding me I am not alone.

—**Lorraine Bossé-Smith**

INTRODUCTION:

Discovering the Hidden Leader Within

Once upon a time, leadership seemed easy. Have a position of authority. Command subordinates. Achieve results. Get greater leadership responsibility. Simple math. Simple subject. The last one hundred years of leadership and organizational life have, however, served to complicate the equation in dramatic fashion. Books on leadership now span everything from the historical "You can learn everything you need to know about leadership from Jesus, Genghis Khan, and Napoleon" to the populist "Leadership is about getting in touch with your inner self and operating in concert with the Tao of the universe."

When I (John) became a leader, I assumed that my position alone would guarantee my success. I quickly learned that positional authority guarantees you blame but does not guarantee you success! I spent my first couple of years in leadership learning quickly that leadership was about *relational influence* more than *positional influence*. Further, most of the things I had learned in my formal training, I would have to unlearn now that I was in actual leadership roles!

Parallel to my personal experience, even with the abundance of leadership resources in our modern era, I have found that clarity has not come to many who are in leadership roles. In fact, confusion abounds as to leadership at a fundamental level. The loss of ethical behavior by many in corporate America (witness Enron, WorldCom, and the like) has led many to question whether we know anything about leadership at all.

As leadership students and practitioners, we bring a simple perspective to the exploration of leadership. *We believe that leadership is about positive and proactive influence in the context of healthy relationships.* Positive and proactive influence is about initiating behaviors that help people to accomplish their personal goals in the context of organizational life. Healthy relationships are about lasting human values lived out in concert with the personalities of the people involved in relationship.

This book will help you form a simple and coherent model of leadership that is relationship driven. We hope to spark a discussion of leadership personality that will free you to discover your personality *and* to learn to cherish the personality traits of others. We will equip present and future leaders to understand how they can be most effective in their leadership roles by operating from their strengths and connecting with the strengths of others. In the end, we will advocate for leaders to be people of integrity and vision living with positive ethical values that influence their relationships. The best leaders are those whom we choose to follow because of *who they are* rather than *what they do* or *what position* on the organizational chart they occupy.

Many have suggested in previous literature that the age of organizations is over. Many have suggested that we have entered into a grand season of personal enlightenment, which renders organizational forms of the past impotent and irrelevant. We beg to differ. We believe that human beings are social creatures. Because of this, we think organizational life and relationship patterns are more important than ever. In an increasingly diverse and multi-faceted society, social networks, and organizational frameworks will assume even greater importance, albeit in different forms than in the past. Strengthening our leadership and relationship skills will make our organizations and social networks stronger and healthier than ever before.

Because leadership operates in the context of human relationships, leaders must be students of themselves as well as students of others. We want to challenge you to consider your leadership capacity. Because leaders influence others, we believe the effort has a "multiplier" effect. Leaders help people to attempt great things they would not do if not challenged. Leadership lifts people to new heights and equips them to think more positively about their present and their future. Be the leader you were meant to be! This book will teach you to lead with integrity, with values, and with character. Learn well and you will leverage your leadership style!

–**Dr. John Jackson**

We have all heard the saying that leaders are born, not made. Certain individuals throughout our history have been elevated to the top of a pedestal because of a certain style of leadership. Our society has typically honored and recognized only this particular style of leadership. We believe that leaders come in a variety of styles. In fact, we have identified four: the Commander, the Coach, the Counselor, and the Conductor. We also believe that each and every one of us has a leader inside just waiting to be set free. How you lead will be greatly impacted by your God-given personality (and certainly what you choose to do with it) and as well as your behavior; however, you *can* be a leader.

For certain people, leading will come easier. This is a fact. Have you ever noticed how some folks are organizational masters? They just ooze with "togetherness." Leadership is similar in that some are naturals and others will need to work at it. Where most people get trapped is in believing that all leaders must act the same way. This book is not about preaching one style of leadership that is the "end all, be all." Conversely, it is designed to help you understand your unique style and how you can contribute to society (professional leadership or personal leadership) based on who you are and how you were designed.

Good leadership is about learning to tap into your strengths, which we all have, and either enhancing those areas you are weaker in or surrounding yourself with others who have what you lack. All of this is with the goal of achieving more together than each person could accomplish on his or her own. Leadership is not a solo act. Ask any quarterback, and he will tell you that the game is won as a team. He may call the plays, but it takes the entire team to make the goal.

Leadership includes directing, inspiring, encouraging, and guiding people to a common destination. Depending upon your personality type, you will rely on one of these more than the others. Good leadership demands more than operating in our comfort zones. Each of us must learn how to minimize our areas of weakness and improve in order to truly be the leader God intended us to be. Jesus is a wonderful example of great leadership as He adapted to the circumstance, becoming just what people needed Him to be at the time. It wasn't fake or manipulative; He was simply ensuring that His communication was received clearly and that His direction was understood. Get ready to rediscover yourself and specifically identify *your* leadership style through a customized assessment. As the authors, we will then show you how you can become a more effective, powerful, and compassionate leader, accomplishing more and building stronger teams in the process.

Don't think you are in a leadership role? Think again. No matter what your position, you are leading people under you, above you, and across from you. John Maxwell calls it "360 Degree Leadership." Even if you are not presently working in outside employment, you still have influence in your home, family, and community. Each of us is called to a unique position that utilizes and uses our specific personality. All leaders do not have to be the same personality style, but all leaders must exemplify courage and willingness to take action.

Are you ready for a journey that will take you to a new level of leadership… one that rallies and motivates your troops to go where they might not dare, left to their own devices? Are you ready to uncover the leader within you that has been patiently waiting to soar? Then read on! Here's to leveraging your leadership style!

–Lorraine Bossé-Smith

CHAPTER ONE

The Lost Art of Leadership

Leadership is an art, not a science. Over one hundred years of leadership writing has brought American society to a fundamental truth: *Leadership is about people...and people are messy!* Today, in the early stages of the twenty-first century, we are learning that leadership is a human endeavor that demands skill and grace not easily learned in educational, corporate, or seminar settings. Good leadership skills are good relationship skills. Leaders who lead well are self-aware and capable of influencing others by the strength of their character and the boldness of their vision. Effective leaders attract followers who are willing to trust them with their vocations and their futures.

In a former leadership setting, I (John) had a rare privilege. The organization was young (less than ten years old), and staffing would typically be a major concern. Of the eight major staff people I worked with on a regular basis (four of whom reported directly to me), I had known three of them for more than twenty years, two of them for more than fifteen years, and one of them for more than ten years. The privilege of relationships built over time allowed me and staff members to develop trust and confidence tested over time and through the journey of life together. The leadership culture that we created, and the decisions we made together, was based on years of trusting and tested relationship investments.

It's About Character

Because leadership is ultimately about character and influence, we believe that every person can exercise some measure of leadership. Leadership may initially be "self" leadership, but it can ultimately expand to influencing others in light of the organic nature of character to "breed" itself in others. Character doesn't stand still...it moves to influence others. Because character influences others, we offer this resource to equip leaders to leverage their leadership style by connecting leadership and personality style in a positive and winsome combination.

Leaders who can adopt this vision of leadership (relational influence and compelling vision) will find themselves consistently building trust and developing relationships that last. My personal tendency is to be very task-oriented. But I realized long ago that no tasks of lasting value are ever accomplished in organizational settings without buy-in of a large number of people in an environment of sustained healthy relationships. In order to leverage their leadership style, you will need to learn your own leadership style (you'll discover that in chapter two and following) and the styles of others. But learning your personal style and those of others will not be helpful unless you commit to building an environment where relationships are valued and relational health is encouraged.

In addition to a commitment to relational health, leaders must also embrace a compelling vision of the future. In the Bible, Isaiah 26:3 (NRSV) says that God "will keep in perfect peace him whose mind is steadfast because he trusts in [God]." This book will help you to measure your success as a leader in light of a firm purpose and a clear vision of your leadership role. We think that success in life comes from mastering specific disciplines and putting those disciplines into play on the field of life.

Have a Clear Purpose

One of the most successful books in history is *The Purpose Driven Life* by Dr. Rick Warren. In his book, he includes a number of key concepts worth our attention: "The purpose of your life is far greater than your own personal fulfillment, your peace of mind, or even your happiness." "It's far greater than your family, your career, or even your wildest dreams and ambitions."[1]

Our understanding of life is that our purpose is found in right relationship to God through Jesus Christ. We believe that when you discover that purpose, it focuses your life and gives meaning and value to your life. When you have clarity of focus, then you can maximize the energy you apply to specific circumstances. Once your vision, focus, and energy are all aligned, we think that life becomes a glorious and grand adventure!

Leaders are Growing People

Leaders are growing people. They begin by growing themselves, and then they grow those around them. Leaders create a growing environment because they have a vision for themselves, their people, and their organizations. The leaders we have been most impressed with over time are those who are growing spiritually, mentally, emotionally, and physically. I (John) have been impressed with many leaders who have continued the discipline of personal growth through the course of their lives. Watching people who grow people has motivated me to be a leader who invests in the lives of others. In our own organization, we regularly invest in training, development, and personal growth for each of our team members. Further, we regularly "benchmark" our organization with other excellent organizations so that we can learn from people and places where growth is taking place.

Investing in Others for Maximum Impact

Leaders invest their lives into the lives of others for maximum impact. One of the paradoxes of leadership is the need to be growing so that you can give yourself away. The more that you give yourself away, the more you need to keep growing so that you can keep giving. The more you grow and give, the more fruitful your leadership harvest will be! Even the Bible says, "You reap whatever you sow"! (Galatians 6:7 NRSV). It is particularly true in human relationships that people who invest themselves in others will never lack for an opportunity to make a positive difference. Robert Schuller, founding pastor and visionary leader of the Crystal Cathedral church in Southern California, told pastors of local churches that "The secret of a growing church is so simple…find the hurt and heal it!"[2] The same is true for leaders: invest your life in others, and you will always have a leadership harvest in the relationships of your life. Those who learn what leveraging your leadership style is all about will have taken the strategic and relational steps to become a peak performer in each of the dimensions that John Maxwell and others have identified for success.

Leadership Practices

Frances Hesselbein, head of the Drucker Foundation (founded by management guru Peter Drucker) and former head of Girl Scouts of America, is one of the keenest observers of the state of leadership research and practice today. In a summary statement about leadership practices, she observed:

> All the effective leaders I have encountered—both those I worked with and those I merely watched—know four simple things:
>
> 1. The only definition of a leader is someone who has followers. Some people are thinkers. Some are prophets. Both roles are important and badly needed. But without followers, there can be no leaders.

2. An effective leader is not someone who is loved or admired. He or she is someone whose followers do the right things. Popularity is not leadership. Results are.

3. Leaders are highly visible. They, therefore, set examples.

4. Leadership is not rank, privileges, titles, or money. It is responsibility.[3]

Hesselbein raises several key issues of "leadership practices" that will be important for readers to lift up in their own leadership experience:

1. **Leaders have followers.** We do not believe this relates to position but rather to influence. John Maxwell regularly says, "Leadership is influence."[4] At the most basic level, we agree. We suggest that good leaders are those who exhibit positive and proactive influence in the context of relationships.

2. **Leaders have a vision of what the "right things" are personally and organizationally.** Leaders we respect and admire are able to capture a clear view of the future and align their actions and the organization's resources in the pursuit of the future vision they see.

3. **Leaders model character and integrity.** More on this later, but we believe that other studies (e.g., Kouzes and Posner, *The Leadership Challenge)* have identified credibility/integrity as the single most important leadership trait.

4. **Leaders accept responsibility for results and consequences.** Leaders don't blame others; instead, they personally shoulder responsibilities and create an environment where others want to be part of the team and to go where the leader takes them.

Leadership Opportunity

Leveraging Your Leadership Style takes the position that the fundamental issue for leadership is not personality style or innate gifts and talents. Each person who has influence in the lives of others has a leadership opportunity. Seizing the leadership opportunities in your life by understanding your own style and the style of others, coupled with a commitment to integrity and a clear vision of a preferable future, will facilitate maximum impact in your leadership life. In our reading of leadership literature and in our personal experiences, we believe the issue of character is a non-negotiable for effective long-term leaders. We know of no single greater leadership quality than this simple issue of leadership character.

All the skills and training in the world will not, over the long haul, overcome a deficiency in character. Further, we believe character is lived out in the context of relationships. Because relationships are where leadership character is tested and demonstrated, we have chosen to focus *Leveraging Your Leadership Style* on the interaction between leaders and people. We do not believe that leadership operates in a vacuum. Leadership is nothing, if not people-driven.

It has been my (John) privilege to work in a variety of non-profit organizations and in the for-profit private enterprise sector for the past thirty-five years. During those years, I've witnessed some amazingly talented people, and many of them have had strength of character and healthy relationship skills to match it. That is an awesome combination! But, tragically, I've also witnessed many wonderfully gifted men and women who had serious character and relational deficiencies. Over the long haul, substantial talent is always ultimately sabotaged by these impediments. To that end, we urge readers to understand the interplay between talent, character, and relationships.

Your Leadership Model

This book will help you form a simple and coherent model of leadership that is relationship-driven. We hope to spark internal and "water-cooler" conversations about leadership that will free you to discover your leadership style and learn to cherish the personality styles of others. At the end of the day, we hope that *Leveraging Your Leadership Style* will be an organic expression of your own self-understanding and your commitment to personal and organizational growth. The time is ripe for a whole new generation of leaders who lead with their heart, their heads, and their hands as servant leaders in positive relationship with those they influence. You were made to be that kind of leader, and we call you to that future.

You were "hard-wired" with a personality that, when properly lived out, enables you to be most effective in your leadership. Your ability to use that personality in conjunction with the personality of others will set your team up for success. *Leveraging Your Leadership Style* is really quite natural. Our hope is that this short book will equip you to develop a synergistic personality and leadership style that flows from who you are. Learning to operate within the context of your divine design will lead to maximum impact for you, the people on your team, and the organization you serve.

CHAPTER TWO
Identifying Your Leadership Style

In the introduction, John and I (Lorraine) shared a bit about the history of leadership and how it has dramatically changed over the years. We believe that the challenges we face in leadership today are forcing us to be better, and we are all for that! For far too long, we have fallen into job descriptions rather than responsibilities. As leaders, we have responsibilities not only to our company but also to each and every person who works for us. If you didn't have a chance to read the introduction, you may want to take a quick look at it (some personalities by their nature skip around, and that is OK; but in this case you may want to go back). Many times, we need to know where we have been in order to see where we need to go.

In the introduction, we briefly touch on the concept of leadership styles. The theory of "leaders are born, not made" doesn't hold water with us. History has too many examples of incredible leaders who weren't of the same cast. In the Bible, Moses had a different approach from Abraham. Deborah was completely different from both of them! Martin Luther King, Jr., influenced people as opposed to Rudolph Giuliani commanding people. Both were incredibly effective, but each man used his unique strengths to accomplish his goals. The list goes on. Coming from very different backgrounds and life experiences, history's leaders have proven to us that we are all created different by God and, therefore, have different abilities and approaches to life. Leadership is no exception. Some people are naturally more comfortable with leadership, but even others who are not as comfortable can still lead effectively. That is precisely our intent with *Leveraging Your Leadership Style*. We not only want you to discover your own unique leadership style but we want you to understand that every person has value, skills, talents, and gifts to offer. Just because someone is different from you doesn't mean they cannot lead. Our society fails to understand this simple point, and many times people are left to feel inadequate on the leadership scale.

Ever watch the *X-Files*? This show is based around two FBI Agents, Mulder and Scully, who are assigned to the "X-File Cases"...those that are strange, bizarre, and unexplainable in nature. A UFO, a suspicious death, aliens—you name it, they have encountered it. Agent Mulder, the male character, believes without seeing. He is a global, outgoing, visual, energetic, charismatic, take-charge kind of guy. Scully, on the other hand, must see things to believe them. Even then, she needs hard-core evidence that is irrefutable. She is more reserved, structured, detail-oriented, quiet, concrete, and cautious. Yet, she is still a leader and an effective one at that. Together, they bring strengths to the team and provide different approaches to solve mysteries. Their differences are what make them dynamic.

A Little History

We believe that everyone possesses the same basic four traits or temperaments, which God gives to us at birth. We have no say in the matter. These four traits are then arranged differently in each of us. Typically, they are called personality traits/styles or human behavior temperaments. Although these personality or human behavior models have been noted since 444 BC[1] and have been defined, labeled, and taught by an array of professionals through the course of history—don't let them intimidate you. They are simply tools for helping us understand each other better and get along with less conflict. These traits are what will help define your leadership style. And speaking of different styles, if you are the impatient kind, feel free to skip ahead and take the assessment! Others will want to take in everything leading up to that assessment. Neither approach is right or wrong . . . just different.

If you were to read one person's work regarding personalities and human behavior, he or she correlates our temperaments with bodily fluids, as observed by Hippocrates.[2] If you study another person's work, the traits are given colors that represent each style—some network marketing companies use this system of categorizing. Still other people have created labels, names, acronyms, etc. in order to help define our personality traits. No matter which schools of thought you are familiar with, they are all attempting to accomplish the same thing: to help you understand how your traits are arranged and how you are different from other people. You see, even though we all have the same four basic temperaments or traits, we each tap into varying degrees of those traits. It is what makes you and not me or someone else. Our unique profile determines how we approach things—everything: communication, conflict resolution, time management, social interaction, and yes, leadership. And because you are different from anybody else, it is important for you to first understand yourself before we talk about your specific leadership qualities. You are embarking on a self-discovery journey that will help you understand how you view things and approach life. It will also guide you through a process of finding your particular leadership style. In the pages that follow, you will discover exactly what your personality profile looks like.

A Bit about Personality Assessments

Some of you may be thinking, "I've taken some of those tests you mentioned before, and I didn't get much out of them." First of all, this isn't a test. No one can pass or fail my BIT (Behavior Individuality Trait) questionnaire. Second, what you will be taking is an assessment, which is basically going to take a snapshot of your personality profile as it reads today. I (Lorraine) have personally designed this assessment with leadership in mind. It will help pinpoint and target certain aspects of your personality design so that you can know exactly what kind of leadership style is right for you. It doesn't mean that you are stuck with this "snapshot" forever, either. We will simply use it for today and for the purposes of this book. You may change in the future, but we will concentrate on today's assessment. Fair enough?

Bit Assessment

Discovering your BIT (Behavior Individuality Trait) is easy by using the following assessment. Remember, no one style is better or worse than the other; they are simply different. God has made each of us unique! There is no one quite like you. Because of this diversity, assessments and tests have been created through the ages to help us understand one another and ourselves better. Basically, we are each a combination of several traits. Each combination is different and determines how we approach challenges, how we interact with people, what pace we take, and how we respond to structure.

Personality or behavior assessments are never intended to be a negative label to be used for judging others or placing them in a box. They do, however, provide incredible insight into how we are wired and how we approach life. As you take this assessment, please keep in mind that our background, upbringing, culture, experiences and faith influence who we become and how we behave as well, which will not be reflected in this particular assessment.

In order to gain the most out of this book, please take the following assessment so that you may discover your BIT. I'll say it again: No one style is better or worse than the other; they are simply different. The assessment won't take long.

Assessment Instructions

Read the following questions and circle the answer that you feel best describes you.

- **DO** be honest and answer each question as you really are. Remember, answers are not right or wrong.
- **DO NOT** answer questions as you would "like to be" or "wish you were." This assessment is only as accurate as your honesty.
- **DO** go with your first response or gut feeling, as it is likely the most accurate.
- **DO NOT** spend a lot of time analyzing, thinking about, or contemplating an answer.

NOTE: If you would answer differently at work versus at home, use work as your reference.

Ready? Here we go . . .

1. **I would describe myself as mostly . . .**
   A. outgoing, but I like to get things done
   B. outgoing, and I like interacting with people
   C. reserved, but I enjoy one-on-one relationships
   D. reserved, and I like systematically analyzing or planning things

2. **If you asked a close friend or family member about me, they would say that I am . . .**
   A. a stable, supportive person
   B. a driven and goal-oriented individual
   C. a cautious, organized individual
   D. an inspirational, fun person

3. **When I have a choice, I like . . .**
   A. a structured, calculated pace with little change
   B. a fast, intense pace and purpose
   C. a fast, high-energy pace with lots of change
   D. a slow, methodical pace with no change

4. **In my opinion, rules . . .**
   A. can be bent or broken; there are too many anyway

B. can help people get along by providing stability and certainty

C. are for other people

D. are necessary for a structured and orderly world

5. **Given a choice, I would prefer to wear . . .**
   A. sharp and classy suits or business attire
   B. tried and true classic clothes that are practical
   C. bright, fun colored outfits that are hip and trendy
   D. calming, subtle-colored clothes that are comfortable

6. **Under stress, I may . . .**
   A. get impatient and bark
   B. retreat to solitude and withdraw emotionally
   C. become quite talkative and disorganized
   D. over analyze and become critical

7. **My life motto is . . .**
   A. everything is done for a reason
   B. go for it!
   C. all for one and one for all!
   D. we need each other

8. **When making decisions, I . . .**
   A. quickly decide and press on
   B. tend to follow popular opinion
   C. ask a close friend what he or she thinks
   D. gather information and research in order to make the right decision.

9. **At a party or large gathering, I am likely to . . .**
   A. find an excuse not to attend; I don't like parties
   B. enjoy mingling and meeting new people
   C. look for a friend or someone I know and usually hang out with just that person
   D. make an appearance, shake some hands, and leave if there is no particular reason for me to be there (or if there isn't anything in it for me)

10. Given a choice, I would prefer to drive . . .
  A. a fast sports car
  B. a reliable, modest mid-size car
  C. a fun, new, and trendy vehicle
  D. a practical, economical car

11. When communicating with others, I tend to . . .
  A. listen more than I talk
  B. state my opinion directly
  C. speak precisely and accurately
  D. talk more than I listen

12. When given a project to complete, I immediately . . .
  A. process and analyze to determine the most strategic course of action
  B. ask questions regarding the time frame, workload, and requirements
  C. delegate with directives
  D. talk it over with others and see who can help

13. When presenting, I rely upon . . .
  A. methodically address concerns and issues raised
  B. quickly get to the bottom line/financial implications
  C. share accomplishments before getting to the facts and figures
  D. provide all facts, figures, and numbers along with forecasts and predictions

14. When presenting, I reply upon . . .
  A. my ability to communicate quickly and effectively
  B. my latest, greatest techy gadget that complements my communication
  C. my PowerPoint® computer presentation that keeps me on track
  D. my slides, charts, graphs, and Excel® spreadsheets to present data

15. I spend the majority of my work day . . .
  A. with the pedal to the medal
  B. reviewing data and formulating strategic plans
  C. motivating, inspiring, and working through my team
  D. meeting one-on-one with staff to ensure everyone is on track

16. When a crisis arises, I will . . .
   A. inform people of the challenge and rally them around it
   B. share the situation with everyone and petition suggestions
   C. stop the bleeding immediately, then determine next steps
   D. refer to policies and procedures on how to respond properly

17. I stay motivated by . . .
   A. doing things correctly and efficiently
   B. working with a team toward a common goal
   C. keeping my focus on the end goal or challenge
   D. encouraging others and receiving warranted recognition

18. When giving performance reviews to employees, I tend to . . .
   A. discuss each and every area needing improvement with kudos last
   B. build up the relationship first then address some minor concerns
   C. provide more encouragement then constructive criticism
   D. not make time for them or rush through with little feedback

19. When I have a great idea, I . . .
   A. get everyone working on it, even if we have to change direction
   B. tell everyone about it without any direction
   C. discuss it with the team and solicit feedback
   D. research and analyze it thoroughly before presenting to anyone

20. When I have a great idea, I . . .
   A. get everyone working on it, even if we have to change direction
   B. tell everyone about it without any direction
   C. discuss it with the team and solicit feedback
   D. research and analyze it thoroughly before presenting to anyone

For some of you, this was a very easy and quick task. You probably only needed a few minutes to complete the assessment. Others, however, may have actually labored over the questions for quite some time. Resist the temptation to go back and change your answers. Accept that it is good enough for today. You can always retake the assessment another time. Remember, we are all different personalities, and no one is better than the other. And we took a snapshot of just today. You are not locked in and bound to this forever. Let's now score your assessment and discover what your BIT profile is.

Scoring Your BIT

Using the blank score sheet on the next page, circle the letter that corresponds with each question. Then count up the number of circles in each column and enter the total at the bottom. The column that contains the highest number is your BIT profile!

NOTE: *If you have two columns that are the same number, review the brief descriptions below, and select the BIT profile you relate with most. You may want to read both of those chapters in order to truly understand your leadership style.*

Example: If you circled letter B in Question #1, then circle letter B on the score sheet. If you circled letter C in Question #2, then circle the letter C, and so forth.

Score Sheet: Find your BIT Profile

Read the descriptions below and determine the one you relate with most often and write it down.

Commander – Congratulations! You most likely tend to be a driven individual who enjoys competition, whether it is with yourself or others. You keep a fast pace and focus on results!

Coach – Congratulations! You most likely tend to be an interactive individual who enjoys people, whether in the company of large or small groups. You are energetic and must have variety.

Counselor – Congratulations! You most likely tend to be a bit on the shy side and enjoy a supportive environment, whether it is at work or at home. You prefer a slower pace and put relationships first.

Conductor – Congratulations! You most likely tend to be a focused individual who enjoys structure, whether it is at work or at home. You analyze before you decide in order to ensure that you will be correct and accurate.

No BIT is better or worse than the other because God made each of us unique. Some leadership traits, however, will help you guide and direct people toward the goal while others will encourage and motivate people. It is all about balance. Remember the example of Jesus? The next chapter will explain more about how you, too, can adapt to the circumstance and be a successful leader.

Remember: No BIT profile is better or worse than another!

Example: If you circled letter "B" in Question #1, then circle letter "B" in the table below. If you circled letter "C" in Question #2, then circle the letter "C," and so forth.

Bit Score Sheet

Q#	Circle Answer			
1	A	B	C	D
2	B	D	A	C
3	B	C	D	A
4	C	A	B	D
5	A	C	D	B
6	A	C	B	D
7	B	C	D	A
8	A	B	C	D
9	D	B	C	A
10	A	C	B	D
11	B	D	A	C
12	C	D	B	A
13	B	C	A	D
14	A	B	C	D
15	A	C	D	B
16	C	A	B	D
17	C	D	B	A
18	C	B	D	A
19	D	C	B	A
20	A	B	C	D
Total				
BIT Profile	**Commander**	**Coach**	**Counselor**	**Conductor**

CHAPTER THREE

Understanding Your Leadership Style

B efore we move on, I (Lorraine) want to be sure you have a handle on how all the personality traits work together to make us individuals. The analogy of a stereo is a great way to explain personality profiles because almost everyone has a stereo of some kind. The volume knob, when turned to the right, increases the volume or indicates a more outgoing personality. Think of louder as more verbal. When turned back to the left, it reflects a quieter, softer, more reserved personality. This represents the world. If you were to divide us, some would be more outgoing while others would be reserved. If we further divided this group, some would be oriented toward "doing things" or tasks while the remaining people would enjoy "being with people."

Volume Control   **Tuner Button**

The tuner knob, on the other hand, points you to a "people" (music) station or a "task" (talk) station. These two knobs divide the world into the personality groups: those who are more verbal, those who carefully select their words, those who tackle tasks, and those who like being around people. Neither group is better than the other. It is simply how the world is divided. God didn't want us to be all the same, so He created four different temperaments. Each of us can relate more with one style over all the others. Your BIT showed you what your primary or most comfortable trait was. How boring the world would be if we were all alike and fell in the same quadrant! Just as a stereo is more complex than just the volume and tuner buttons, so is your personality. You don't stay put and only use one of the four temperaments provided. You may have related most with the Coach BIT, but you will visit the other traits in the course of a normal day. Each of the styles identified above has traits associated with it that enables us to accomplish things: make decisions, interact with people, handle change, and manage details. I like to take the stereo analogy further to describe how we can flow from one to the other.

Personality Panel

Most cars today have stereos with equalizers. An equalizer is used to change the output of the music to fit a particular style of music or a person's individual taste. The newer cars have electronic ones that automatically arrange the tones to the type of music selected, such as country versus pop or rock. The older models have levers. Each lever is pushed up or down to achieve the specific sound you want. We also have the ability to change our output, regardless of our style. With a car stereo, if you want more bass, you push that lever up. If you desire less treble, you move it down. You continue moving the levers until you find just the right "balance" you wish to have for your music. We each have a similar arrangement going on in what I call our "Personality Panel." Like the stereo equalizer, our Personality Panel enables us to take our four standard traits and change them to reflect our situation, circumstance, or desire. In other words, you are wired to respond, communicate, and behave in one manner more often, but you have the ability to adapt as necessary. In fact, for good leadership, it is mandatory. The four main levers are: **Decision** (noted by Commander people), **Interaction** (a trait of Coach folks), **Cadence** (important to Counselors), and **Details** (a gift of Conductor individuals). Since God made us a certain way, we are preprogrammed with each area at a certain level. Again, your preprogramming is what makes you unique from anybody else. You might be higher in the Counselor style and prefer a slower cadence, lower in the Commander, making you more contemplative, and average in the Conductor or details trait. We all have different levels, and we are targeting your primary personality trait in this book. However, you are able to, just like on a stereo, move or retrieve more or less of each trait as you deem necessary. It takes more energy for us to "visit" other areas, but we can do it. As we grow and mature through the journey of life, we typically get better at balancing or softening out the rough edges.

Any personality trait off the chart or pushed too far becomes a negative, not a positive. Ever hear someone's car come "booming" by, and you think your chest will cave in from the pounding? When people have only the bass turned up to the max, it distorts the music. Music was intended to be a blend of sounds, just as we are a mix of traits. Besides sounding obnoxious, if you were to push the bass lever to the max, for instance, you would eventually blow out your car speakers. The stereo system was not designed to handle such an extreme, and neither are we. Here is an example of a individual Personality Panels. They associate best with the Commander temperament because that is their highest score or trait. They are able to blend well and have fun and enjoy a faster pace, unlike a person who is a higher Counselor temperament. They can handle details when needed, but don't have a passion for them.

Personality Panel

COMMANDER (Decision)	COACH (Interactive)	COUNSELOR (Cadence)	CONDUCTOR (Details)
Alone	High	Slow Pace	Concrete
Together	Low	Fast Pace	Abstract

Adapting with Style

Looking back at your assessment score, which trait do you find easier to use than the others? Below are descriptions of the areas we can visit to adapt as necessary:

Decision—Commander people are known for their ability to make quick decisions. This trait determines how you make assessments and decide. The higher your score or the higher you raise the lever, the quicker you will respond and the more likely you will not petition the help of others. The lower the score or lever (not less, just different), the more time you will take to assess matters, and you will include input from a team of people you trust, as the Counselor people will do. You use this trait every day to assess and make decisions. You are constantly moving the lever up and down to accommodate the situation, but you will feel most comfortable here if your style is Commander. You definitely like to be in charge!

Interaction—Coach people are gifted at communicating with others. This trait determines your interaction with people. The higher your score, the more social and public you are with people. You enjoy high-energy conversations and large gatherings. The lower the score (again, not less just a different measurement), the more reserved and quiet you are; and you prefer private, small groups as opposed to large public ones, like Conductor individuals. You use this trait every day because you can't get away from people—they are everywhere! So, in order to appropriately handle situations you face, you already raise and lower this accordingly. Coach people, however, love living here. You easily work through a team of people, inspiring and motivating them to great heights.

Cadence—Counselor people strive for stability. This trait determines the pace at which you take in life. The higher your score in this particular area means the slower you prefer to approach life. You probably don't like much change and typically respond well to routines. The lower the score in this case, the faster the pace you prefer, like the Commander types. One cadence is not better than the other. You move this lever up and down as needed as well. Some people might be "speed demons" when it comes to work, but they may tap into this trait when it comes to their relationships with family and friends because they want to slow down and enjoy the moment. Overall, you will feel most comfortable taking a slower pace if you are a Counselor. You support others in their attempts to accomplish their tasks.

Details—Conductor folks love being correct. This trait determines how you approach rules and structure. The higher your score, the more structure you strive to obtain. The lower the score, the less likely you are to follow the rules. Every time you arrive at a destination, attend a meeting, pick up food at the grocery store, and balance your checkbook, you are raising this quadrant up because it requires details. You are constantly using this trait throughout the course of the day to accomplish tasks. If you are a Conductor, you are comfortable staying here and working hard on systems that provide structure to the team.

Keep Growing

No matter what your BIT style, you are a mix of all four: Deciding, Interaction, Cadence, and Details. You see, although you will primarily operate out of one temperament more frequently than the others, God created you with the ability to access all four traits. In fact, life requires that you use all four, but we each vary the degree, level, and frequency at which we will utilize those temperaments. If it seems like I'm hammering this point, well, I am! Some schools of thought do not believe that we can adapt and change; we are simply what we are, and that is it. I say that's hogwash! Life demands us to be flexible, and we must balance a variety of things that require different aspects of our personality. I want you to understand that you are not permanently stuck without any hope of growing. Life is all about growing. Stop growing, and you die. For leadership, it is paramount to continue growing— if we are to be successful, anyway. As a leader, you have mastered this ability to "wear many hats," but you may have not understood why some things are easier for you than others. I hope it is all coming together for you.

Each of us has a comfort zone, and that is our primary BIT. We do not expend a lot of energy living in this area. Those who are high in the detail trait (Conductor) find enjoyment in creating systems, but those who are lower in that category must work harder at it. They can certainly perform the same tasks, but they will exert more effort to accomplish them. Make sense? Throughout the book, we will refer to your particular BIT style (Commander, Coach, Counselor, Conductor) and how it relates to leadership, but now you have a deeper appreciation for how all the traits work together.

Because it is so important, we will state again that no BIT profile is better or worse than another. These BIT profiles are not designed in any way to put you in a box or label you. On the contrary, we are hoping to open your eyes to a wider selection of options that will work for you, and at the same time, help you understand that others are different. Too often, we tend to think that everyone should operate just like we do. We have lived with our style for so long that it is easy to think it is the only way. Not so! God knew what He was doing. He has made the world a beautiful blend of all sorts of personalities. Could you imagine if we were all alike? Not only would the world be boring, but depending upon the personality style, it could be scary!

Leadership Examples

Look at the Bible and the people Jesus chose to surround Himself with. He selected a variety of personalities:

- Paul was a Commander type, very decisive and direct
- Peter was a Coach, influencing and inspiring
- Luke was a Counselor, compassionate and stable
- Matthew was a Conductor, detailed and precise

Jesus had a balanced team, and we need balance as well. The more you understand and develop your leadership style, the better equipped you will be to surround yourself with the right team and to tap into their strengths.

Warning: Discovering your style is not a license to say, "This is just the way I am," and it certainly doesn't give us the right to be harsh, cold, or insensitive to others. As a business consultant, I (Lorraine) have encountered too many companies where the boss thinks his staff has communication issues, when the reality is that he is lacking the ability to adapt to other styles. Help is on the way for you to lead with style and to maximize your impact!

> *"[Effective] communication does not begin with being understood but with first understanding others."*
>
> —W. Steven Brown[1]

CHAPTER FOUR
The Commander

Leader of the Pack

Commanders believe in their ability to connect the "known" of today with the "unexplored" of tomorrow. Commanders see people, projects, resources, and strategies as vehicles to reach the untapped potential of the future. Some of the greatest leaders in history have been Commanders. The Commander leadership style is well known, well documented, and well understood. Most of us long for Commanders to lead our organization, as long as we don't rely upon them for friendship! This leadership style has clear upsides and huge potential pitfalls, particularly given the increasingly desperate need for authentic relationships that exists in American society.

In previous generations, it may have been enough to lead others by a "Commanding" style simply based on one's position in the organizational hierarchy, but such is clearly no longer the case. The Commander leader of today must know how to shape his or her team, cultivate the potential of each team member, and build the chemistry of the whole group for maximum success. NBA coach Pat Riley has done well to utilize his Commander leadership styles to work with high-capacity team members for maximum success (though even here with these famous coaches we see the obvious blending of the styles as they work with high-capacity players and teams). While Commander leaders of today understand the critical nature of working with and through teams of people to achieve maximum success, they still recognize their individual responsibility for results. Coach Bo Schembechler tells about the third game of the 1970 season. His University of Michigan Wolverines were playing Texas A&M, and they could not move the ball. All of a sudden, Dan Dierdorf, their offensive lineman—who was probably the best in the country at that time—came rushing over to the sidelines. Fed up with the team's performance, he yelled at Schembechler in front of everybody on the sidelines. "Listen, Coach! Run every play over me! Over me! Every play!"[1] And they did. Michigan ran off-tackle six times in a row and marched right down the field. Michigan won the game.

Commanders are willing to risk for the future because of their fundamental belief in their preferred view of the future. Where other leadership styles may be willing to live with incremental and gradual change, Commanders are willing to seize the future. This is your destiny; this is your contribution. If you are a Commander, you cannot abide simply "doing laps" or doing the same thing over and over again. You know that tomorrow is brighter than today, and you are ready to seize the opportunity in spite of the risk because you believe in the payoff and the worth of the adventure.

Commander Profile

Commanders take responsibility for results, not only that they themselves produce but that are derived from the successful sharing of responsibility. The article titled, "Management by Walking Away,"[2] reports on successful Quad/Graphics: "We don't believe that responsibility should be that defined," CEO Quadracci explains: "We think it should be assumed and shared. Nothing should ever be somebody else's responsibility. Anybody who sees that something needs to be done ought to assume responsibility for doing it."

In an earlier book titled *PastorPreneur*, I (John) wrote this about Commanders:

> The Commander enjoys taking risks because he (or she) sees them
> as necessary for progress. This person envisions big goals and
> marshals the troops to accomplish them. He is practical and logi-
> cal in outlining the steps to get where he wants to go. In volunteer
> organizations such as churches, Commanders need to understand
> that not everybody is goal-oriented. Many people feel threatened
> by risk, so a wise Commander takes time to inform, motivate, and
> encourage those with whom he works.[3]

Commanders are able to envision the future and imagine what would happen if all the resources of people, programs, and property were aligned to accomplish the vision. Andy Stanley, pastor of Northpoint Community Church in Atlanta, describes his practice this way: "Several years ago, I printed out the following question and stationed it in a prominent place in my study so I would be forced to read it every day: *What do I believe is impossible to do in my field...but if it could be done, would fundamentally change my business?"[4]*

Commanders, fundamentally, are clear about the future. Their primary contribution to the organizational task is to see the future, describe it with clarity, and passionately pursue the future potential even when others give up. Commanders are likely to move forward even when consensus is hard to muster.

Many of our teams and workforces are like the family that had become fed up with the noise and traffic of the city and decided to move to the country to try life in the wide-open spaces. Intending to raise cattle, they bought a western ranch. Some friends came to visit a month later and asked them what they had named the ranch. The father said, "Well, I wanted to call it the Flying W, and my wife wanted to call it the Suzy Q. But one of our sons liked the Bar J, and the other preferred the Lazy Y. So we compromised and called it the Flying W, Suzy Q, Bar J, Lazy Y Ranch." Their friend asked, "Well, where are your cattle?" The man replied, "We don't have any. None of them survived the branding!"

Leveraging Your Leadership Style as a Commander

Leveraging your leadership style means people who are hard-wired as Commanders live out of their strength zone. They marshal resources, make the vision clear, and motivate others to sacrifice on behalf of the vision. As they do this, they learn to value the values of teammates as well. Team members are not viewed as tools to accomplish the vision but as partners in the vision itself. Commander-style leaders need to recognize the importance of empowering others and calling forth the best possible effort and energy from their teammates. Commander leaders must demonstrate their leadership strength by making sure that the vision is clear, shared by the team, and then lead by example as they demonstrate their personal commitment to the vision and the team. Rick Warren says, "If you want to know the temperature of your organization, put a thermometer in the leader's mouth."[5] Commanders are the organizational thermometers most known, seen, and watched by the organizational community.

Organizations need Commander-style leaders. Commanders provide the "driver" component that organizations need to pull the organization and team into the future. The challenge for Commanders is to develop the capacity to work with teammates in a way that enriches each individual person and cultivates the ability of the team to work with synergy and strength in order to accomplish organizational goals. Effective Commanders learn how to marry the unleashing of personal potential with the vision of the organization so that personal and corporate goals are accomplished together. James Crook wrote, "A man who wants to lead an orchestra must turn his back on the crowd."[6] Leaders turn their backs on the crowd and follow their mission no matter what the crowd thinks. Commanders passionately pursue their vision even when swimming upstream.

Other Commanders

Are you a Commander? Is that how you are hard-wired? If so, you love taking risks for the sake of accomplishing great things for your organization. You see the future and bring it into the present. *But,* you must learn to work *with* people and teammates and not *over* or *around* them! Commanders who learn to envision, empower, equip, and energize their circle of relationships will be well on their way to leveraging your leadership style. If you do, you will be in good company. Some well- known effective Commanders:

- Margaret Thatcher, former Prime Minister of England
- General George Patton, US Army
- Bill Gates, Microsoft
- Bill Hybels, Willow Creek Community Church
- Mary Kay Ash, May Kay Cosmetics Company

Commanders sometimes see the time necessary to involve others in the vision process as "wasted time." Learning to work with the other leadership styles requires the Commander to master the art of negotiating between personality and work style differences as a fundamental part of the leadership task. Working with other leaders is not a diminishing of the power of vision; rather it is testing the power of the vision to reach into the soul and leadership styles of others.

Cautions for Commanders

Commander-style leaders must monitor their task orientation to ensure that they do not cut short the need of each of the other styles to be in meaningful relationship. If you are a Commander-style leader, be sure that teammates get quality time and that you are consistently investing in relationship with your primary team leaders.

Commander-style leaders also need to carefully create a culture where risk is rewarded and, just as importantly, failure is not fatal. Commanders are accustomed to going for the "big goal" and, therefore, have generally come to grips with the inevitability of failure on the road to success. Unfortunately, Commanders are often such driven persons that they can create environments where other leadership styles fear introducing new ideas if failure is a distinct possibility. Commanders must reward reasonable risk in order to produce an innovative culture.

Finally, Commander-style leaders need to be exceedingly clear about the interaction between their values and their vision. Commanders are often so vision driven that they have a "disconnect" when it comes to living out real values. People and organizations are shaped by values; Commanders who are so driven by their vision of the future that they are willing to transgress the stated values of the organization will find themselves alone in their quest to see the vision accomplished. Commanders who live out their lives and leadership with integrity must ensure that their vision and values are both aligned and consistently lived out in relationship with others.

Communicating for Maximum Impact

Commanders who are effective in their leadership learn how to communicate with other leadership styles for high impact. Part of mastering the art of leadership is learning how to lead across the spectrum of styles and circumstances. Commanders typically have no problem cultivating passion for their vision of the preferred future. Communicating that vision requires the creative capacity to understand the worldview of the other styles. When communicating with a Coach, it is critical to focus on their dreams and the dreams of others and to develop a plan that is motivational and inspirational. Communicating with a Counselor requires attention to individual goals and providing an environment of security and stability. Conductors require direct communication with a clear analytical approach that is supported with action plans and structure to accomplish the vision.

Commander leaders learn to communicate with attention to individual styles, and they learn to communicate consistently and repetitively. Many Commander-style leaders find it easy to believe that "I said it once, and that should be enough!" Truthfully, vision has to be communicated repeatedly in order for it to take root in the soil of the soul of team members. Rick Warren says, "Vision leaks." He's right. Effective Commander leaders learn how to communicate creatively, contextually, and consistently for the sake of the vision. Leveraging your leadership style requires Commanders to master communicating vision, developing leaders who can seize and see the vision along with them, and network relationships for the sake of seeing the future become reality today!

Commanders see the future, seize the future, and secure the future. They believe in the power of promise and are willing to risk greatly for the hope of tomorrow. Commanders passionately believe in the hope of tomorrow; those they lead are then willing to place their trust and lives in their leadership.

> *"Once a spiritual leader is sure of the will of God, he will go into immediate action, regardless of consequences. He must be willing to accept full responsibility for consequent failure or success and not place on a subordinate any blame that might accrue."*

> —J. Oswald Sanders[7]

CHAPTER FIVE
The Coach

Call Me Coach

Did you see the movie *Miracle* with Kurt Russell? Besides being an awesome true story, it has an inspirational and motivating message: We can do it! If you haven't seen it, let me give you the "Reader's Digest" version. In the early 1980s, the USA forms, for the first time ever, an Olympic hockey team. Kurt Russell's role is the coach, who persuades the "powers that be" to embark on such an endeavor, even though the Russians own this event, bar none. He is given the task of pulling together the right team for the job. He gathers young boys from all over the country to try out for the team. Throughout the movie, you see very talented and capable hockey players. What finally brings the team together, creates unity, and gives them the passion and drive to win is their coach. Kurt Russell hardly ever hits the ice. What he does do is inspire, influence, and motivate his players to be their best and work as a team. Without ruining the ending for you, they win! This is the role of a Coach.

I'm assuming you discovered that you related best with the Coach after taking the BIT assessment in chapter two. I encourage you to read chapter three because it gives you greater insight into how you can understand and motivate others. But this chapter is especially for you, the Coach! You will learn more about your leadership style and how to develop other areas of your personality in order to truly be the leader of influence you desire to be. The more you understand yourself, the better equipped you will be to lead others and be successful, professionally and personally.

Coach Profile

Here's what being a coach means: You are gifted with people. You are high energy and enjoy working through a team. In fact, you are the master at fostering team spirit and getting everyone on board as well as excited.

As a leader, you are persuasive and have the ability to help people accept your viewpoint or opinion without coming across as forceful. You are a global, big picture thinker and as a result, details are not your strong suit. You are a strong starter but may have difficulty finishing a task, especially if it isn't very much fun. You make up for this with your incredible enthusiasm. You are truly great at motivating your troops. But leadership is more than being a cheerleader. You must also provide strength, guidance, and direction to your team, unlike this story:

A man got a dog and established rules:

1. The dog is not allowed in the house.
2. Okay, the dog is allowed in the house, but only at certain times.
3. The dog is allowed in all rooms, but has to stay off the furniture.
4. The dog can get on the old furniture only.
5. Fine, the dog is allowed on all the furniture, but is not allowed to sleep with the humans in bed.
6. Okay, the dog is allowed on the bed by invitation only.
7. The dog can sleep on the bed whenever he wants, but not under the covers.
8. The dog can sleep under the covers by invitation only.
9. The dog can sleep under the covers every night.
10. Humans must ask permission to sleep under the covers with the dog.[1]

You've Got Style!

Instead of the AOL® slogan "You've got mail," I'd say, "You've got style!" Coaches are definitely not short on personality. Coaches are never speechless. They have plenty to say, and usually do so with emotion. Leadership requires them to say and do some tough things that may not go over well with everyone; and for a Coach, that can be challenging. Coaches are outgoing and social. Because of this, they want to get along, be accepted, fit in, and keep peace.

Coaches may also have trouble with hard and fast rules. Like the story above, they are more comfortable changing the rules to suit the occasion. As a leader, you need to be the one defining the parameters and helping others work within them. Pushing the envelope is an excellent trait, but keep things in perspective. Know when it is okay to "ask for forgiveness later," but know when you really should ask for permission first.

Coaches are a whirl of mental activity and rarely completely shut down. They are a creative force that can certainly energize those around them; but they need to be careful, because they can also burn out! Since Coaches are fast-paced, they can be hard to keep up with for other personality types. Coaches can't impose the same standards on their employees who may not be as high energy as they. They need to remember to respect other's pace and style. Besides, others balance the coach, and that is what a team is all about.

If you are a Coach, you are a passionate person. When you are up, you are flying high; when you are down, however, you have a black cloud looming over your head. Regardless of your mood, you have difficulty masking it; and everyone knows how you feel. Although it can be appropriate at times to spew your feelings to your peers, I caution you to hold back when around your staff. Never complain down. Your team is seeking balance and security in the work place. Emotional outbursts or casting blame, another trait of Coaches, can scare them. Even though you may quickly recover, their perception of you will be altered for some time.

Patron: *Waiter! My soup has a fly in it!*

Waiter: *Try again. Maybe the fly will disappear.*

Patron: *No, it is still in my soup.*

Waiter: *Maybe it is the way you are eating the soup; try a fork instead.*

Patron: *Even when I use a fork, my soup still has a fly!*

Waiter: *Maybe you ordered the wrong soup.*

Coaches must work at controlling inner emotions and staying focused on the task. Their motto is, "If it ain't fun, why do it?" Leadership will demand more from them, so concentrating on short-term engagements and projects that involve creative energy and fun people will soften the blow and set everyone up for success. Coaches are great at initiating change, creating new products, and starting new endeavors. Leave the maintenance to those on your team who are gifted at it. You don't have to be the best at everything.

Other Coaches

Ensure your team has a mix of styles that will compliment, support, and challenge you. You can spot other Coaches by listening. These folks talk, talk, and talk! They are not quiet and shy. In fact, you can probably hear them laughing up a storm several offices down at work. They usually have the latest joke to share or an exciting story to tell from their weekend. Coaches are not afraid to try new things and typically wear trendy clothes that are bright and colorful. Keep these visuals in mind with your customers and clients. The more you know, the better you can negotiate and serve.

Chances are Coaches will drive a flashy automobile that is the latest hip ride in town. It won't be white; no, it has to be a bold color. They are usually the drivers that go really fast for a while and then all of a sudden slow down to a crawl in the left lane. Sound familiar? It is easy for Coaches to get engulfed in a really juicy conversation and lose their focus while driving. They probably have no clue that anyone else is on the road with them; and when they do, they will just smile and wave.

Remember that Coaches normally have a short attention span because of their fast pace. Although they really want to listen to you, they are more excited about sharing their thoughts with you. They can have difficulty focusing on your words because they are formulating their next thought.

Their office might look like a bomb went off. Keeping things orderly and clean isn't fun, so why bother? As long as they feel they have some sort of system that works for them, it isn't a priority. As a leader, remember to focus on the "end result" rather than "how to get there." Since you operate in a similar mode as other Coaches, you shouldn't have much difficulty being flexible here.

Coaches don't really have an in-between mode. They have the "high acceleration" gear (or pedal to the metal) and the "stop" (drop dead) gear. Again, try not to impose this pace on everyone. I once had a boss who worked until 1 a.m. every day and expected all of us to do that—not!

Other Coaches are John Maxwell, Bill Clinton, Frances Hesselbein (Girl Scouts of America), John Wooden, Jeffrey Immelt (GE), and Elizabeth Dole.

Cautions for Coaches

I know you typically don't like to hear about limitations or what you can't do because it isn't much fun, but Coaches can get in trouble by talking too much and not listening enough. Someone once said, "Winners listen while losers just wait for their turn to talk." Dominating conversations will only shut others out and prevent unity. In order to build your team up, you will need to listen more. Concentrate on the other person's feelings and on relating to them. Work at slowing down, listening first and speaking second. The older I (Lorraine) have gotten, the more I have noticed that successful people do more listening than they do talking. The more insecure a person is and the more they are nervous or uncertain about themselves, the more they talk. Keep this in mind the next time you have a meeting. You'll be amazed at what you learn about someone by listening.

Because you tend to express your feelings, you can sometimes let go inappropriately. As I mentioned earlier, make sure you express yourself to the right people. Show your staff the positive side, and keep the really negative garbage for the leadership team. I love the movie *Saving Private Ryan* with Tom Hanks. Remember the scene where one of his troop members asks, "Why don't you complain, sir?" Tom Hank's character replies, "Because stuff doesn't flow downward. You complain to me, and I talk to my superiors." I don't know if it hit you as hard as it did me when he finally broke down alone and cried, but often times as leaders we don't have someone to go to. We certainly should not put our burdens on our team. This is one of the responsibilities of a leader, no matter what your style.

Your ability to persuade people is truly a gift. As the saying goes, you could probably sell a block of ice to an Eskimo! If you are passionate about it and excited about its potential, you will be fired up. Just be cautious not to overdo it or push too hard. Used car salesmen get a bad rap for being "over the top." Many movies have a main character that is despised because he or she went too far, pushing away everyone, like Jim Carey in *Liar, Liar*. Since you desire to build unity within your team, tone it down for your staff.

Coaches are great at pouring themselves into a project at the beginning, but can lose interest quickly and move on to something else, struggling to finish what they first started. This is not only dangerous; it is destructive to you, the Coach; your career; your goals and your relationships. You are never short on ideas, but you also must balance that with actual accomplishments. Talking about something isn't doing it.

Talking about something isn't doing it. Take action!

Take action and make a commitment to finish. Another way to beat procrastination for the Coach is to understand what you are putting at risk as a result of your inability to perform. You are losing respect and will continue to do so until you live up to your word. Trust is so easily broken and takes a very long time to rebuild. Don't blow it, but think things through.

Communicate with Style!

As a Coach, your communication style is informal and friendly. As a leader, however, you will need to communicate to all styles. Because you are a very talkative person, you may not always notice how quiet others are being. You are so enthusiastic and energetic that you can talk for long periods and lose track of time. Although sharing is one of your strengths, be aware that everyone is not like you. Commanders want to know "What is in it for them" right away with no delays. They are bottom-line people. They may have a hard time listening to your stories. In fact, they may even cut you off. Give them some slack and understand that they aren't a "conversation connoisseur" like you, and don't take it personally. Get to the point quickly. You can always ask them if they want more details, but give them the choice. Counselors are much quieter and won't interrupt you.

Try not to dominate the conversation and allow them to speak by asking questions that draw them in. One of the ladies in my Executive Forum Group is an energetic Coach. She almost has to cover her mouth at meetings to prevent from being the first one to speak all the time. We all appreciate her efforts and welcome her ideas when she speaks. Her attempt to respect other styles has made us appreciate her more.

So when you ask a question, give others time to respond. Don't answer your own question with another story! Conductors eat, drink, and sleep details, so they will want to exchange those specifics with you. Appreciate the structure and order that they provide and try to speak their language the best you can by sticking to business. Below are some tips for each profile that will help you communicate with style:

Commander—When talking with a Commander, be direct and to the point. They will appreciate your getting right to the bottom line. No need to "break the ice" or socialize with Commanders. Use words and phrases that are results oriented and answer the question "What is in it for me?" which is foremost on their mind. Most Commanders do not like being told what to do. They prefer options and deciding for themselves, so don't tell them what to do, but offer suggestions that are results-oriented and challenging. If you have details or stories to share, simply ask them, "May I share this with you?" This way, you get their permission and their undivided attention. You both win.

Coach—When interacting with other Coaches, be you! You are speaking with other folks who love a good story. Laughing it up with this group is what it is all about. Details will not be the focal point, so if you do need to get an answer, gently guide and lead them back on track. This may be difficult for you since you enjoy a good conversation, but you will know how to motivate others to respond since you are an influencer!

Counselor—When you are communicating with Counselors, s-l-o-w down. Don't interrupt them, even if they seem to take a while to respond. Give them the time they need to formulate their thoughts. For a Coach, it may seem like an eternity, and you have so much to say; but be sensitive to their thoughts and feelings. A friendly, soft approach that affirms them works best. If you are too verbal with your communication, they will retreat, withdraw, and shut down. The problem is that you will probably not notice because they will not say anything to you. Don't assume silence is acceptance and admiration of your verbal skills. Be in tune to their body posture, facial expressions, and "temperature." Remember, they love people like you, but they show it in a quieter manner.

Conductor—When engaging with a Conductor, give 'em "just the facts, ma'am, just the facts." Picture in your mind Sergeant Friday, and you have a pretty good idea who you are dealing with—your opposite. Again, you will want to slow down and allow them time to process. In fact, you may need to give them additional time to think things over before they respond. Don't be disorganized or too personal, but systematically present your case or idea.

Lead with Style!

Coaches truly bring life to an organization. Without their creativity and energy, a company's mission or product line can die on the vine. Their enthusiasm and zest for "going for it" is contagious. As a Coach, use your charisma to influence and inspire others to go for greatness, but remember to always balance it with integrity and sincerity.

> *"There are countless ways of attaining greatness,*
> *but any road to reaching one's maximum potential must be*
> *built on a bedrock of respect for the individual,*
> *a commitment to excellence, and a rejection to mediocrity."*

— Buck Rogers[2]

CHAPTER SIX
The Counselor

Each leadership style has a different starting point. But effective use of the leadership style has the same ending point: People fulfilled in their personal experience of growth, and the organization accomplishing its goals and dreams with satisfied workers and customers. Knowing where each style begins can help you to understand what "worldview" that style operates under. In brief, Commanders start with the vision of the future, Coaches start with the vision of the team, Counselors start with the vision of the individual, and Conductors start with the vision of the system.

It's All About Relationships

Welcome, Counselors! You care deeply about others, about how they feel, what they experience, and whether they fulfill their personal sense of destiny. Counselors have an innate desire to make sure that their relationships are stable and that tasks are accomplished within a supportive environment. Counselors do not think that the end justifies the means. In fact, most Counselors believe that the means are the end. In other words, if the means (relationships and supportive environments for people to flourish) are right, the ends will naturally follow!

Counselors are particularly equipped to provide support for others in a different way from Coaches. Coaches provide a supportive framework for teams of people to operate, but do so within a clear vision of what the team can accomplish. Counselors start with the individual and not with the team. Counselors provide a framework for people to operate within that equips them to fulfill their individual destiny, and that is their primary concern. If you are a Counselor reading this chapter, then you are passionate about people experiencing health from your leadership. Good Counselor leaders are loved by those who follow them.

Counselors are strategic in their approach to individuals. They care about what happens to the feelings, focus, and future of individuals. They are not like Lucy from the comic strip *Peanuts*, standing with her hands on her hips and shouting out a long list of Charlie Brown's many failures and inadequacies.

Communicate, Communicate, Communicate

The critical leadership task for a Counselor is to rightly connect the heartbeat and emotional strength of the individual to the mission and vision of the organization. Most Counselors will do this well by helping individual stakeholders to "connect the dots" between their personal emotive make-up and the goals of the organization. Counselors are naturally good with process and do well to assure that team members understand how their unique personality contributes to the overall design of the team. If you are a Counselor, working hard to encourage that people not only experience "acceptance" but also experience "success" will endear those in your organization to you.

Counselors work hard to guarantee that relational bonds are clear and strong and that they are investing in the personal development of those for whom they are either responsible to supervise or are in relationship with. My (John) experience with Counselors is that they are wonderful personal coaches, they make great trainers, and they are the people you want to go to when you need some truthful and encouraging words. They do, however, have some potential areas of struggle when it comes to leadership. The first has to do with communication. Communication is the key to productive relationships and a supportive environment. Many of us know the importance of communication in marriage, perhaps because we've seen or heard this kind of (mis)communication:

"Why do you want a divorce?" the judge asked. "On what grounds?"

"All over. We have an acre and a half," responded the woman.

"No, no," said the judge. "Do you have a grudge?"

"Yes sir. Fits two cars."

"I need a reason for the divorce," said the judge impatiently. "Does he beat you up?"

"Oh no, I'm up at six every day to do my exercises. He gets up later."

"Please," said the exasperated judge. "What is the reason you want a divorce?"

"Oh," she replied. "We can't seem to communicate with each other."

Leading with Courage

The second arena of difficulty for the Counselor is difficulty itself. Many Counselors prefer to avoid confrontation with individuals and can become paralyzed by organizational stress and tension. My encouragement to you as a Counselor is to focus on helping each stakeholder to recognize the importance of both their personality and the goals and mission of the organization. Rather than be defeated by difficulty and criticism, instead consider the predictable nature of criticism. If you are doing something worthwhile, someone will always criticize you. In fact, the philosopher Aristotle observed, "If you don't like criticism, do nothing, say nothing, be nothing." Instead of fearing criticism and difficulty, recognize that criticism and difficulty often bring up opportunities for change. In fact, it is my understanding that the Chinese characters for crisis and opportunity are just one small stroke apart.

Perhaps you've faced difficulty that has derailed you before. If so, this parable might be of interest to you as you discern the difference between crisis and opportunity:

> *A Canadian bird decided that it was too much trouble to fly south for the winter. He said to himself, "I can brave a winter. A lot of other animals do it. It just can't be that hard." So as all the other birds flocked away toward sunny South America, he stayed behind and waited for winter.*

> *By the end of November, he was having serious second thoughts. He had never been so cold, and he couldn't find any food. Finally, he broke down and realized that if he didn't get out of there soon, he wasn't going to make it. So he started flying south all by himself. After a while, it began to rain. And before he knew it, the water was turning to ice on his wings. Struggling, he recognized that he couldn't fly any longer. He knew he was about to die, so he glided down and made his last landing, crashing to the ground in a barnyard.*

> *As he lay there stunned, a cow came by, stepped over him, and dropped a plop right on him. He was totally disgusted. "Here I am," he thought, freezing to death. "I'm about to die. I'm on my last breath, and then this! What an awful way to go." So the bird held his breath and prepared to die.*

But after about two minutes, he discovered a miracle was happening. He was warming up. The ice on his wings was melting. His muscles were thawing out. His blood was flowing again. He realized he was going to make it after all. He got so excited and happy that he began to sing a glorious song.

At that moment, the farm's old tomcat was lying in the hayloft in the barn, and he heard the bird singing. He couldn't believe it; he hadn't heard anything like it for months, and he said to himself, "Is that a bird? I thought they'd all gone south for the winter."

He came out of the barn, and lo and behold, it was the bird. The cat crossed over to where he was, pulled him gently out of the cow plop, cleaned him off, and ate him.

Three morals to this story are: (1) Not everyone who drops a plop on you is your enemy; (2) Not everyone who takes a plop off you is your friend; and (3) If somebody does drop a plop on you, keep your mouth shut![1]

Interacting with Other Styles

Counselors, like all other styles, often find themselves engaged in relationships with others who are wired up with a different style. In each case, Counselors will find it helpful to understand the leadership style of the other person and to work accordingly with them. Thankfully, it has been my (John) experience that Counselors are the most adaptable of the leadership styles.

Commanders are future focused and generally driven by results. So Counselors who are working with Commanders need to be able to state their concerns or objectives in terms of the future results that will be accomplished and how a suggested course of action regarding a project or person helps to fulfill the mission of the organization. Commanders are most uncomfortable with organizational relationships that appear to have no "forward motion" in them.

Coaches are team focused and are driven by the strategic interactions of the players. Counselors who want to be effective with Coaches will work toward helping Coaches understand how greater attention to individual characteristics and needs will actually benefit the team. Counselors are often helpful to Coaches who can sometimes be blindsided by their perception of team unity when they have missed signals of an unfulfilled team member. Counselors help Coaches to see the team through a series of individual lenses.

Conductors want to know that the system is designed for efficiency and effectiveness. Conductors need Counselors to help them understand the human "variables" of their system design. If you are a Counselor working with a Conductor, your best bet is to ensure that you both are clear about what the organization is trying to accomplish. Second, focus on how human interactions are part of any well-designed system, and assist the Conductor to see the importance of healthy human relationships in an efficient environment. Conductors are most frustrated with Counselors who are unable or unwilling to link the "human factor" to the system design. Counselors who help bridge the system design to the human environment provide the context for healthy relationships within the organizational system. People like former President Jimmy Carter, Fred (Mr.) Rogers, Nancy Reagan, and former NBA coach Phil Jackson all have used their Counselor styles with great impact.

Leveraging Your Leadership Style

The other types will consistently challenge Counselors who choose to live out their leadership style in an organization. Most of these challenges will come regarding whether the Counselor is most concerned with the organization or the individual. The best answer is yes! Counselors are concerned about both because they recognize no dynamic organization will thrive without a healthy relational environment. At the end of the day, all organizations connect people together for the sake of organizational health, and Counselors help individuals to be healthy parts of the team. Counselors are like the farmer in this story:

> *A man was driving a little too fast on a wet road and slid into a ditch. A farmer came by with his horse named Duke and offered to pull the man's car out of the drainage ditch.*
>
> *The farmer hitched his horse to the car and said, "Pull, Bill, pull!" His horse named Duke did not budge.*
>
> *Then the farmer said, "Pull, Sadie, pull!" His horse still didn't move.*

Finally the farmer cried, "Pull, Duke, pull!" The massive horse lunged forward and effortlessly pulled the car out of the ditch.

The distressed motorist, filled with gratitude, thanked the farmer, and then asked, "Why did you call your horse the wrong name twice?" "My horse is blind," explained the farmer, "and if he thought he was the only horse pulling, he would not even try."

Good Counselors practice continuous improvement in their own leadership style and in their interactions with others. Even a strong and respected corporate leader like Jeff Immelt, CEO of GE, recognizes this when he describes his own practice: "Leadership is an intense journey into yourself. You can use your own style to get anything done. It's about being self-aware. Every morning, I look in the mirror and say, 'I could have done three things better yesterday.'"[2]

CHAPTER SEVEN

The Conductor

Just the Facts

I (Lorraine) know you took the assessment in chapter two and read about your profile in chapter three. You learned basic principles about the different personality styles and how each of us is created uniquely. You probably highlighted some things, made some notes and are ready to apply your new knowledge to your leadership role. I know this because you are a Conductor, and that is my second trait. Although I am fast-paced and decisive, I do want to do it right—the first time. I have found that my detailed nature has served me well through the years. When team members cast visions, share dreams, and have big ideas, Conductors can begin to formulate in their head an immediate strategy for how we will make it all happen. If you have ever been told "You rained on my parade" or "You are always so pessimistic," then you are doing the same thing—seeing obstacles along the path. You are taking words and looking for a way to turn them into a reality. This is a great gift but can be seen as a negative to other personalities such as the Commander and Coach. What Conductors need to learn is timing.

The title character in the television show, Monk, is off the charts on the Conductor scale. Like any strength, when it is pushed too far, it becomes a negative. He can indeed be too much. However, he also brings incredible talents to his work. Every team needs a Conductor. And Conductors can be awesome leaders when they learn how to use their systematic approach to life to benefit others while at the same time benefiting from the often "random" approach of other leadership styles.

This chapter is for you. Specifics on how you can lead, communicate, interact, motivate, and succeed will be provided so that you can analyze it, process it, and make your own decisions as to how you will want to incorporate it into your own life. As the author, I ask that you keep an open mind. Conductors love to gather information, so consider this yet another research project. I don't expect you to take everything we say as the absolute truth for you, but I do hope that you will consider trying some new approaches. It has been said that the definition of insanity is doing the same thing over and over again but expecting different results. Conductors can get in a rut and do things because they have always been done that way. From one Conductor to another, check your negative opinions at the door (at least until you have a chance to take this all in, assess it, and decide for yourself) and read your chapter with a spirit willing to learn. So let's dive into some of the details about your profile.

The Conductor Profile

Some readers will remember Sergeant Friday of the television show *Dragnet*, and his motto, "Just the facts, Ma'am, just the facts." Conductors prefer working on tasks due to their reserved and detailed nature. It doesn't mean they can't stand people or can't work with them. Refer to the radio dial analogy in chapter three. Conductors simply tend to tune in toward the tasks rather than the talk. Your relationships are much more private and one-on-one. My mother was very private with her feelings and her faith. If you didn't get to know her intimately, you might never see her "soft side." Conductors protect their feelings and keep things close to the vest until a person has earned their respect or trust. Thus, you may not have a high volume of people you let "in" and get to know intimately, but those you do, you are very close to.

When a Conductor speaks, it is clear and concise, which serves you well in leadership—no messing around. You typically won't ramble and will stick to business, which the Commanders greatly appreciate. Conductors as leaders create an environment that is structured and organized because they don't enjoy chaos, especially when it could have been prevented with a little planning. In fact, this can actually tick you off! Something every Conductor has to learn is: Everyone is not like you. And here's a nugget for you that made a world of difference for me: People don't do things to you; they do what they *know* and are who they are.

People don't DO things to you;
They do what they know and are who they are.

Your lack of patience for disarray and disorganization can create tension with your team members, especially the Coaches. Although you aim for perfection in just about everything you do and accuracy is a must for you, remember to focus on the end goal, which is ultimately what matters. Your peers and team members may approach things differently. You are the one others look to in order to confirm accuracy and correctness, so use this gift when communicating the objective. This way, everyone knows where he or she is supposed to end up.

Your leadership style establishes rules, laws, and procedures because you know that they provide structure and create a dependable environment. You believe in and support proven and traditional methods, especially when you have confirmed them with your own analysis. Don't allow this to prevent you from taking advantage of opportunities. Leaders must balance research, risk, responsibility, and results. Too much of one will wreak havoc.

Conductor leaders find comfort in facts and figures. You love calculating, measuring, and attempting to prove or disprove just about anything. You are analytical by nature. To some, however, you can come across as cold and heartless. On the contrary, you are a very caring individual. The more you value something or someone, the more research you will conduct. You want things right. It is paramount that you let your team members understand this key point: You *do* care. Don't get so wrapped up in the "things" of business that you forget the "people."

Watch your stress levels because you can actually become quite critical and cold. You don't mean to be, but you retreat to what is most comfortable for you—we all do. You are a disciplined, loyal, hard-working individual, so tap into those strengths at times when you need them to get you through.

Birds of a Feather

Other Conductors will come to you with a point or key question that is right on the mark. They may often be quiet, but they will come forward when the situation warrants it. They prefer to work on projects and may go it alone or participate on a team, depending upon what is appropriate for the situation. Since you come from the same mold, give the specifics and let them "do their thing." Just ensure that they do not become paralyzed by the analysis. I've found the best way to prevent this is to set a deadline for the research aspect of the project. Then, action must be taken. All the data in the world is useless without action!

All the data in the world is useless without action!

Your Conductor comrades may have difficulty working with the Commanders on the team, seeing them as pushy. They may also get frustrated with the grand visions from the Coaches. Help your teammates understand that without these players, we would have nothing to work on. A team takes all personalities.

Wondering who may be Conductors in your life? They usually wear "classic" colors and outfits that never go out of style. They will select clothes that are proper for the situation, meaning that they will never be over-dressed or under-dressed for the occasion. Most likely, they are wearing glasses because they are practical. Since they spend so much time conducting extensive research, they use their eyes more than most. They will wear jewelry, but it will be minimal and appropriate for the event. Chances are they are driving a very practical car that meets their specific needs at this time. If they have children, for instance, then they are driving a minivan that will accommodate those needs. If they commute, then they will have something smaller and more economical. Their vehicle will be a tried-and-true color or whatever they could get on sale. Most of the time they will honor all traffic rules and regulations to the letter of the law, unless a situation warrants "bending the rules just this once."

Is your office organized and clean, everything in its place? Conductors tend to have logical filing systems and thoughtful placements for key equipment. If they have pictures from home, they will be close to their chair. Anything out or on the walls will be clean, not cluttered. Bookshelves will be organized either alphabetically or by size to keep the shelf clean and clutter-free. But keep this in mind: Conductors can get overwhelmed and stuck in the details and forget to stick their head up. Be cautious as a leader to look up once in a while. Your troops will need you to rally around them and not just "do" tasks.

Conductors are very strategic leaders. This is an immense contribution to any organization, and don't forget it! If you relate best with this profile, then you are in good company with Al Gore, Stephen Covey, Steven Sample (former President of USC), Hillary Clinton, and most engineers and lawyers!

Stephen R. Covey reminds leaders in his best-selling book, *The 7 Habits of Highly Effective People,* to identify our priorities:

- Pick the future, not the past.

- Focus on opportunity rather than a problem.

- Choose your own direction rather than climb on the bandwagon.

- Aim high, aim for something that will make a difference instead of something that is safe and easy to do.

Stephen R. Covey also reminds leaders about relationships: "From the foundation of character, we build and maintain Win/Win relationships. The trust, the

Emotional Bank Account, is the essence of Win/Win. Without trust, the best we can do is compromise; without trust, we lack the credibility for open, mutual learning and communication and real creativity."[1]

Something to Consider

Just remember that people make the company. Although it may be a challenge for you, try to focus on the person and not the data. The Coaches are your complete opposite and will require the most effort on your part. One way to improve relationships with them is to be more open and honest about your feelings. Switch from discussing "things" and begin sharing thoughts and feelings, and you will warm right up to them. Leaders must wear many hats. It isn't being deceitful but rather flexible. Again, this may take some work, but you can do it!

New Company Policy: Effective Immediately

Sickness: We will no longer accept a doctor's statement as proof of sickness. If you are able to go to the doctor, you are able to come to work.

Operations: Operations are now banned. As long as you are an employee here, you need all that you have. You should not consider removing anything. We hired you intact. To have something removed constitutes a breach of employment.

Death of Others: This is no excuse for missing work. There is nothing you can do for dead friends, relatives or coworkers. Every effort should be made to have non-employees attend to the arrangements. In rare cases, where employee involvement is necessary, the funeral should be scheduled in the late afternoon—we will be glad to allow you to work through your lunch hour and subsequently leave one hour early, provided your share of the work is enough to keep the job going in your absence.

Your Own Death: This will be accepted as an excuse. However, we require at least two weeks' notice as it is your duty to train your replacement.

Restroom use: Entirely too much time is being spent in the restroom. In the future, we will follow the practice of going in alphabetical order. For instance, those whose names begin with 'A' will go from 8:00 to 8:10, employees whose names begin with 'B' will go from 8:10 to 8:20 and so on. If you're unable to go at your time, it will be necessary to wait until the next day when your time comes again. In extreme emergencies employees may swap their time with a coworker. This exchange must be approved by both employees' supervisors.

Thank you for your loyalty to our company. We are here to provide a positive employment experience. All questions, comments, concerns, complaints, frustrations, irritations, aggravations, insinuations, allegations, accusations, contemplations, consternations, or input should be directed elsewhere. Have a nice week.

—The Management[2]

Early in my career, I leaned so heavily upon the Conductor side of my personality that I began to impose my high standards on others. I expected way too much of others who were not the same personality, and it stressed us all out. Accepting what someone gives when it isn't how you would do it is tough, but if you want to build bridges and a strong, healthy team, then you must master this concept. You must learn to focus on the human element, not just the task element. What is the end goal? Don't lose sight of what is important. Being "right" is not always the right path to choose.

As I matured as a leader, I realized that allowing people to work in their own style got me greater results than forcing them to be like me. One of my female employees was truly disorganized. Her office was a disaster (from my point of view),but yet, she always managed to do her job extremely well. I could have gotten upset over the "how" but chose to celebrate her accomplishments. Everyone won! Leaders want to win, no matter what their personality—that's the fact! Go for what will get everyone the furthest and toward your goal the quickest.

When everyone is on board and doing their job correctly, amazing things can happen. Don't avoid changes or new projects because you aren't familiar with them. This is called procrastination and can cause you intense pain, frustration ,and disappointment. It can also prevent you from doing things right and on time.

Instead, enjoy the journey of growing and learning something new. Knowing you, it won't take you long before you are a real pro at it. Let me say a word about perfectionism: It cannot be obtained. Excellence, on the other hand, is doing our very best. It is accepting that this is good enough for this particular project at this particular time in these particular circumstances. When you strive for excellence, you are focusing on the end result. Conductors need to understand that they will never have all the data or all the time in the world; action is required. If you find yourself stuck, take some steps immediately to get momentum going again.

Victory goes to the one who will not quit!

The Right Stuff

Every team has a blend of personalities. As a Conductor, you will most likely have no issue with the Commanders because they are businesslike, just like you. Your Counselors are soft spoken and easygoing, and you will find them enjoyable to work with. As I mentioned before, the Coaches will be your biggest challenge. And as a leader, look at this as an opportunity to grow. Your communication style is slow, thoughtful, and precise. You spend time listening and processing what you hear before you will speak. On the contrary, Coaches speak first before thinking. You probably believe in giving each person time to talk because you believe it is polite. Well, if you wait on the Coach to stop speaking, you could wait a very long time!

As a leader, you will need to engage more with the Coaches and refrain from being too logical. Gather details throughout the conversation in a friendly manner. I know this sounds a bit intimidating because you would like extra time to formulate your thoughts and feelings; but having the right information too late makes it wrong, and nobody wins.

Although you can relate with the Commanders, they are much faster than you and want to know what is in it for them right away with no delays. They are bottom-line people, and it will behoove you to give them brief statements rather than all the details. Get to the point quickly. A successful strategy here is to give the down-and-dirty immediately to Commanders and then ask, "Would you like me to expand on this?" If they say, "Yes," then you have permission to go deeper. And, you have their undivided attention. If they say, "No," then leave it at that. Push your need for details upon them. Look for windows of opportunities to share more data and take them, but don't force it.

As I said before, you will appreciate a Counselor's structure and order and shouldn't have too much difficulty speaking their language. Just remember that they are warmer and friendlier than you come across. Try to break the ice before you dive into business.

The Right Leader

Life requires every personality and leadership style. Particular organizations need certain types of leaders due to the nature of their business. As a Conductor, you may find yourself in the tech industry or medical profession. Perhaps you oversee engineers because you are suited quite well to work with these individuals. But you can lead anywhere or anyone, with a little work.

> *I can accept failure. Everybody fails at something.*
> *But I cannot accept not trying.*

Visiting is a powerful word when it comes to the different aspects of our personalities. I challenge you to ask yourself in every situation what would be the "right" thing to say or do, then do it! Tap into those parts of your personality, even if they aren't your strengths or favorites. Keep in mind that you do not have to live here; you are simply visiting for the moment because it is the right thing to do.

Tap into your nature of wanting to be correct, and you can be a master of adapting to any situation—and succeeding at it. Make it a goal to invest into your people: their lives, career, and success, and you will reap enormous rewards. You can't go wrong with that.

> *"If you don't change, you don't grow. If we don't grow we are not really living.*
> *Growth demands a temporary surrender of security."*
>
> —Gail Sheehy[3]

CHAPTER EIGHT
Model Team Leadership with Style

Peter Drucker has long been recognized as the "Dean of American Management." His death in 2006 caused many to review his legacy of sixty-plus years of writing. For me (John) personally, one of his most helpful works was *The Effective Executive*. In that book, Drucker outlines five disciplines of the mind that an effective executive has to practice. Those five practices are presented here in summary form:

1. Know and control where your time goes to the greatest extent possible.

2. Focus on outward contributions you can make in terms of results rather than focusing on techniques or tools.

3. Build on the personal strengths [what Drucker called elsewhere, "islands of health"] of those you work with. Build on what you can do well.

4. Concentrate on a few major areas where superior performance will produce outstanding results. Do first things first and second things not at all.

5. Make effective decisions. Systems and strategies must be sound and decisions made to support wise choices in each dimension.[1]

Even now as I reread the list many years after its publication, I am impressed with how clear Drucker was—and how difficult it is to live out that list! In fact, I'm betting you may be depressed right now as you realize how many times you have neglected that simple list of five things! Thinking about how you can effectively leverage your leadership style with your teams really comes out of number 3 above. You and your co-workers can build a healthier and more productive team that accomplishes world- class results by focusing on a few basic practices. And since that list of five things from Drucker was hard to grasp, how about if I shorten the list to four things that you can do to leverage your strengths and those around you?

Build Dynamic Teams

I have written elsewhere[2] about building teams through four specific practices:

1. **Healthy Relationships.** While many in the business context will respond that it is either impossible or inappropriate to develop relationships with co-workers outside the work environment, we both want to contend against that notion. Even if you never become a social companion of those you work with, we believe it is imperative to build healthy relationships with co-workers. The more you understand of the personal life circumstances of your co-workers, the more equipped you are to support them in their work environment. Understanding the background and at least the personal and family circumstances of your co-workers will help you to invest in their development and growth. Every time I've had a leadership failure, it has been due, at least in part, to a disconnect between the personal circumstances of the employee and the aims and goals of the organization I was leading. Patrick Lencioni's work on *Five Dysfunctions of a Team* provides a helpful framework to assist each of the leadership styles to create a healthy relationship experience.

2. **Training.** Specific skill training for team members in accordance with their leadership style will enable them to become more productive and build upon their own strengths. Since vision is always more "caught" than "taught," the process of training often provides great vision-refining moments. The teams at the church I led (cvcwired.com) attended at least one to two key training events together each year. The experience of these events confirms and supports the individual leadership styles of the participants. We have often had the positive experience of varying leadership styles experiencing a training event from their varying perspectives. Utilizing that shared experience and learning to communicate the values and training tools among the several styles has been a productive experience that leads to enhanced understanding of one another.

3. **Benchmarking.** Exposing your leadership team to greatness has great value. Visiting other organizations in similar industries helps to elevate the thinking of everyone involved. Each of the leadership styles will experience this from different perspectives, but in ways that will be invaluable to your team. Conductors will learn new systems, Counselors will develop deeper insight into effective human behavior, Coaches will learn how high-performance

teams operate effectively in dynamic organizations, and Commanders will become even more passionate about clear vision!

Both Jim Collins (author of *Good to Great*) and John Maxwell talk about "levels" of leadership. My experience suggests that we must teach people that leadership is a process, not an event. Helping team members see their leadership potential unfold over time is part of the process of effective equipping. I encourage organizations to provide "first step" opportunities for those who want to begin the process of developing their leadership capacity as well as the developmental path for "high capacity" leaders who can effectively lead other leaders. Benchmarking other organizations helps to keep each leadership level growing. A leader—whatever his or her leadership style—who is not learning is not leading for long.

4. **Leaders Teaching Other Leaders.** Growing up your leadership team is not a solo sport! It is a long held maxim of the training cycle that:

- You watch me do it

- We do it together

- I watch you do it

- You teach someone else how to do it

Teams that perform well over time teach emerging leaders of all styles how to interact and work with other styles and how to develop other leaders who do not share their leadership style.

Develop and Equip Leaders

Understanding how to function in teams is a critical skill for effective leaders in our day. Laurence Haughton, author of *It's Not What You Say...It's What You Do*, has written about the key importance of healthy teams functioning in organizations; consider the following:

- Eighty-three percent of business problems are caused internally, not by depressions, recessions or earthquakes.

- Execution of ideas and plans breaks down because of:
  A) Expectations are not clearly communicated
  B) They don't fit the right people to the objectives.

- When you match the right person to the right objective, you double your chances of success of execution!

These observations push us to the brink! We simply must develop other leaders and equip leaders to become effective parts of a cohesive and forward directed team. When leaders have reached a point of maturity on the journey of leadership development, it is imperative that they begin developing other leaders. Once they have basic skills mastered, leaders learn best by teaching others. This is equally true for each of the leadership styles, but perhaps is most difficult for the Commanders. Commanders are, by nature "big picture" people. You will need to help Commanders understand the "what and how" of their leadership arenas so that they can communicate to others. Most Coaches are "wired" from the start to equip other leaders; in fact, this is perhaps their strongest natural skill set. Counselors will require additional assistance in extrapolating from the personal focus to the organizational application (this is a consistent theme with Counselors). Conductors may have to "dummy down" their natural systems orientation as they categorize and summarize training to communicate effectively with the other styles.

Create Healthy Teams

These four practices form the heartbeat of a developing and healthy team. John Maxwell wrote about Mary Kay Ash, the founder of the Mary Kay Cosmetics Company. In an article in his weekly newsletter (see injoy.com to sign up for that newsletter), he offers the following information about all people.[3] These observations will be most helpful to Conductors as they understand that people are really complex systems, so if Conductors can relate to people as they do to complex environments and systems, they both will be more effective as they strengthen and support those around them. Here are John Maxwell's basic observations about people:

1. Everybody wants to be somebody.

2. Nobody cares how much you know until they know how much you care.

3. Everybody needs somebody.

4. Anybody who helps somebody influences a lot of somebodies.

5. Today, somebody will rise up and become somebody.

Leaders are Learners!

You would think, of all the organizations we can imagine, that churches would be the very best at this particular aspect of leadership. However, Thom Ranier, in a study published in November of 2004[4] indicated that number three in the top five lists of weaknesses that pastors listed was dealing with staff. Most of those surveyed considered their staff leadership skills to be weak, and virtually all were able to cite poor decisions in their history of organizational leadership that revolved around staff and team leadership. It is our hope that *Leveraging Your Leadership Style* proves to be accessible and helpful to leaders, pastoral, and otherwise, who want to improve their leadership of teams.

Those who have a passion for learning usually realize they are deficient in some area. That sense of need drives them to read, to study, and to ask questions. They aren't satisfied with things the way they are, and they long to learn so they can fill the gaps in their own understanding. Their goal is not knowledge for the sake of knowledge. Rather, knowledge becomes a tool to accomplish change.

In his outstanding book, *The 7 Habits of Highly Successful People*, Steven Covey wrote of the necessity of "sharpening your saw,"[5] —keeping an edge mentally, emotionally, spiritually, and relationally so we don't become dull and ineffective. Almost three millennia ago, King Solomon wrote:

> *"If the ax is dull and its edge unsharpened,*
> *more strength is needed*
> *but skill will bring success."*
> (Ecclesiastes 10:10)

When a lumberjack or carpenter notices that his saw isn't cutting well, he has a choice to make. He can keep cutting with the increasingly dull blade, and he will have to expend more effort and take more time to get the job done. Or he can stop for a few minutes, take out his file, and focus his attention on making his saw sharper and more effective. Has he wasted these minutes filing his saw? He certainly hasn't cut any wood during that time, but those minutes are an investment that pays great dividends in time and effort over the next hour or so.

Sharp Leaders

Some of our more experienced readers have probably flown on a cattle car. If you have, you were probably greeted by friendly airline personnel and might have been sung a little song by a flight attendant. If you've flown Southwest Airlines, you've flown the only continuously profitable airline of the last few decades. What has made Southwest so successful? The People—plain and simple. Southwest (SWA) is about putting people first. In fact, their training center is called, "People University." SWA employees are evaluated annually using an appraisal document that reinforces the company's focus on people, its culture, and values. A full 40 percent of the evaluation has to do with leadership and embodying the Southwest Spirit. Southwest's commitment to customer service is legendary (southwest.com/assets/pdfs/corporate-commitments/customer-service-commitment.pdf), and the "spirit" of Southwest is a core part of how each employee is evaluated. Effective leaders can learn from the Southwest example!

Some of us became dull months or years ago. In fact, it's been so long that we don't even know where to look for the file! But we need to find one and do whatever it takes to become sharp again. "Sharp" people are excited about God's calling. They have read the latest articles and books, and they are eager to share what they are learning. Sharpened leaders are eager to try new things, and their enthusiasm is infectious to those around them. These leaders have learned to value the file as much as the saw because it makes them far more effective. Entrepreneurs must keep growing and learning or else they simply are not entrepreneurs for long.

> *"Perhaps the biggest reason*
> *for the movement toward empowered work teams*
> *is the fact that teams work."*

> —Richard S. Wellins[6]

CHAPTER NINE
Mentoring with Style

Through this book, my (Lorraine) hope is that you have not only learned about yourself but about others as well. Leadership is about building bridges, and in order to do that, we must step outside of ourselves and into another's shoes. Our personality assessment is a great tool for that! You can immediately identify a person's primary mode of operation and begin adapting to meet his or her specific requirements. And by applying what you know about others, you can truly be a great leader.

In the dedication, I mention two such leaders who made a positive impact on my life through their leadership style. Besides challenging me while at the same time encouraging me to be my very best, they took the time to mentor me. Mentoring is a critical step in developing leaders because it takes the "head" knowledge and moves it into practice. The world is full of books on leadership. We probably can't read them all in our lifetime. All of that knowledge won't amount to a hill of beans, however, unless we apply it, try it, and customize it to fit our unique personality/leadership style.

The Timothy, Paul, and Barnabus Principle

I am a tennis player. I love the game! I've been playing since I was a teenager. Through the years, I have made a concerted effort to play with people more skilled than me. Although I may not be able to win the entire set, I am improving my game with each stroke…if I pay attention and learn from my mistakes. I have also ensured that I include some games with players who aren't to my level yet because they build my confidence. On the court, I can try new strategies and form with little or no risk. To balance it all out, I then play with my peers where we have no clue who will win because we are so evenly matched. These keep me sharp and on the ball (okay, pun intended) at all times, requiring keen mental alertness and physical strength. In leadership, we are wise to follow this example called the Timothy, Paul, and Barnabus Principle.

The Bible teaches us, and actually instructs us, to have a person of each level in our life for completeness: growth, confidence, and giving. Do you have a mentor? Are you a mentor? In my dealings with corporate executives, I hear how overloaded and overworked they are trying to climb the ladder or simply stay afloat. Many of them can't be bothered with such an endeavor. Well, I'm here to tell you that you can't afford not to!

As leaders, if we do not invest in the lives (and careers) of others, then we have failed miserably at our responsibility. Our people look to us for guidance, motivation, support, encouragement, and assistance along life's path. If you don't like the job description, then don't take the job.

Responsibility

I often hear movie stars getting upset over being photographed in a magazine or complaining that they cannot live a normal life. Maybe I am heartless, but my feeling is that they signed up for the job; deal with it! Hollywood has been this way forever, and it isn't going to change. Become famous, and you sacrifice your privacy. Granted, some media have stepped over the line, and that is entirely a different story. But to be angry at "what is" is simply absurd. Leadership is no different. If you embark on this journey, then you have responsibilities to others. Period.

Some leaders of late have not performed well in this department, and many lives have suffered as a consequence. We must take the role as leader very serious and attempt to be all that God wants us to be for the sake of all others.

The wise learn from their mistakes;
those who are wiser learn from the mistakes of others.

Share What You Know

Mentoring isn't just about sharing head knowledge but in our day-to-day actions. Ask any parent, and they completely comprehend that children learn more from what they see than what they hear. Parents are modeling behaviors and beliefs for their children every minute, and so it goes with leaders. Our actions speak volumes. What is your team capturing from you? Are your actions aligned with your mission statement and company objectives?

Simple things like taking a lunch break once in a while or going home at reasonable times does model balance to your team. I know you love what you do and/or feel pressure to put in long days, but you need to show your people that you have a life…and that it matters. They need to be given the "OK" to make their home life a priority. If you press hard and create a warp-speed approach to everything, your team will follow…or worse, burn out. Leadership is a marathon, not a sprint! Keep your long-range goals and objectives in mind and remember that you will need your people to be strong for the long haul.

Mentoring does take time, I won't lie to you. The time you do spend, though, will be well spent. Nowhere else will you receive such a return on your investment each and every time. You cannot go wrong in investing in someone else, even if they choose not to apply what you have shared.

Give of Yourself

Mentoring can also be exhausting. Giving of yourself does take energy, but you will never feel so fulfilled. With any team I have had the honor of leading, my goal has been to learn their individual dreams and aspirations and how we can make them happen together…all the while accomplishing company goals and objectives. I am a performance-driven individual who wants to succeed, but I saw modeled that when your team succeeds on an individual level, everyone wins. Each time you help a teammate grow, your relationships get stronger, and their loyalty deepens. People will work harder and longer for you because they want to versus working because they have to.

Take pride and joy in helping someone move to the next level of his or her career. Yes, you may lose some people, but you have made a difference in a person's life. I believe that comes back to you in a richness you can't put a price tag on. Leadership really is selfless. Movie can make it look like you can be a self-serving, get-everything-you-want-and-be-a-total-jerk, but that is far from the truth. It is hard work…but oh so rewarding when done right.

In the end, we are known only by the impact we have on others.

Expand Your Mind

When we rise to the level of leadership we have always dreamed about, we think we have finally arrived. I laugh at myself for thinking this for even a nano second. The reality is, it has just begun! Sure, you may get that office with a view and the responsibility you feel you can handle, but you haven't stopped growing… at least I hope you haven't. Someone once said, "The day you stop learning is the day you die!" Leaders are learners. I believe it is paramount for leaders to have a mentor, no matter what his or her level. We all need someone in our life who has accomplished great things and is at a level we aspire (this can be spiritually, mentally, physically, professionally, personally) to be one day. These people have wise words and often plenty of encouragement. They are hard to find, but you don't always have to have a one-on-one relationship with them.

I've often used people I admire and respect as my role models without them knowing. I then make sure I have people to confide in and bounce ideas off of in my life. In your position, I'm sure you have very few people you can trust with your innermost feelings and thoughts. Yet, you must have such a person in order to be a healthy individual and successful leader. I'm a facilitator for a group called Executive Forums. They are a national organization, and their mission is to help you! Check them out at ExecutiveForums.com and see if your area has a group. Here, you will find peers as well as mentors. And, you will benefit both professionally and personally, guaranteed.

The Gift of Giving

If you are new to taking on a mentorship role, I believe you will thoroughly enjoy it so much you'll continue doing it the rest of your life...even when you retire. It is addictive because when you give, you see, you actually receive. It is a most wonderful gift and blessing to assist another person.

I have always been a giver but had difficulty accepting what others would give me. I finally realized one day that if I denied a person a gift, I got in the way of God's work. They couldn't be blessed if I didn't allow them to give. Mentoring is the same way. You have to give but also receive. In both cases, people will be blessed. Now maybe your life is so perfect that you do not need additional blessings, but I'll take whatever I can get! Seriously consider mentoring. Chances are you already are mentoring those on your staff. You wouldn't be in your position if you hadn't taken the time to invest in them.

Often our roles in leadership provide incredible opportunities for us. I love the movie *A Knight's Tale* with Heath Ledger. One of my favorite lines is when the MC introduces Sir Ulrichstine before the lancing battle. He is a Coach and really woos the audience with his animated storytelling. He approaches the knight and says, "I got their attention; now you win their hearts." Your role does not guarantee you a high-impact team, but mentoring will. How can you not have a dynamic, engaged team when you are investing in each person?

Pass It On

If you still aren't convinced that mentoring is worth the effort then consider this: We teach what we know and reproduce who we are. The older we get, we tend to realize that life is short. Our mothers warned us! We begin to think in terms of "What do I want to leave behind?" At the same time, the word "legacy" becomes more surreal and meaningful.

Promise Keepers swept the country some years ago, bringing men together to better themselves. These days their conferences are held on a smaller, more strategic scale, but their message still remains: No Regrets. I've lost both of my parents already. They were much too young. God gave me many lessons out of this, but one of the most profound was living every day right. When the sun sets, I don't want a single person in my life to wonder if I love them. If I conduct myself properly, they know without a doubt how I feel. Life boils down to relationships, even at work. What will you leave behind?

CONCLUSION:
Leveraging Your Leadership Style!

The Parable of the Blind Men and the Elephant

It was six men of Indostan, to learning much inclined, who went to see the elephant, though all of them were blind, that each by observation might satisfy his mind.

The first approached the elephant, and happening to fall against his broad and sturdy side, at once began to bawl: "God bless me! But the elephant is very like a wall!"

The second, feeling of the tusk, cried, "Ho! What have we here so very round and smooth and sharp? To me 'tis very clear this wonder of an elephant is very like a spear!"

The third approached the animal and happening to take the squirming trunk within his hands thus boldly up he spoke: "I see, the elephant is very like a snake!"

The fourth reached out an eager hand and felt about the knee: "What most this wondrous beast is like is very plain," quoth he: "'Tis clear enough the elephant is very like a tree! The fifth who chanced to touch the ear, said "E'en the blindest man can tell what this resembles most; deny the fact who can, this marvel of an elephant is very like a fan!"

The sixth no sooner had begun about the beast to grope than seizing on the swinging tail that fell within his scope. "I see," quoth him, "The elephant is very like a rope!"

And so these men of Indostan disputed loud and long, each in his own opinion exceeding stiff and strong. Though each was partly in the right, they all were in the wrong!

—John Godfrey Saxe[1]

Unfortunately, more than we'd like to admit, Commanders, Coaches, Counselors, and Conductors often resemble the six men of Indostan! *Leveraging Your Leadership Style* was written to help all of us take a step back and see the "elephants" of our lives with greater clarity. Having a clear vision that helps us understand that people are our greatest resource and learning to maximize our own strengths and support each of the other styles is what *Leveraging* is all about. It has been our deepest hope and prayer that you've gained better understanding of your own personality and how you might leverage your leadership style in relationship to team members who have other personality styles.

As we conclude, I (John) want to advocate for some bold challenges. Take matters seriously. Get focused on your team and learn who they are, how they are wired and how you can help them become their very best for their sake and the sake of the organization. Robert Cooper, in his book, *The Other 90%: How to Unlock Your Vast Untapped Potential for Leadership and Life*, said the following:

> *Say no to the drug of gradualness.* It was Martin Luther King, Jr., who spoke out strongly against making slow changes. Either we risk or we don't, he said. Either we change or we don't. There is no acceptable middle ground because it lulls us into complacency. Lasting changes rarely occur when we ease our way into the future. They come when we leap. The leaps themselves can be small or large. Once we take action, we see things differently and for many of us, there's no going back. Leaders enable others to act. They foster collaboration and build spirited teams. They actively involve others. Leaders understand that mutual respect is what sustains extraordinary efforts; they strive to create an atmosphere of trust, and human dignity. They strengthen others by sharing information and providing choice. They give their own power away, making each person feel capable and powerful.[2]

We want to advocate for making a bold choice. Can you decide, having read this book, *that you will become a leader who focuses on having positive and proactive influence in the context of healthy relationships?* I am increasingly convinced that every level of leader/manager and employee in any organization should be able to leverage his/her influence in the lives of others. Recently, an article from the *Globe & Mail* quoted a Canadian Conference Board report which suggested that every level of management and leadership in an organization affects the future, including, and perhaps most importantly, the middle manager level:

> Carolyn Clark, Vice President of Human Resources for Toronto-based Fairmont Hotels & Resorts Inc., said in an interview that a growing body of research shows "People don't quit their companies; they quit their managers."[3]

In recent years, work/life research done in a variety of settings has consistently shown that a supportive manager is more valued by employees than anything else the organization can offer, the study says.

Leveraging Your Leadership Style provides a helpful tool to equip yourself and those in your organization for the future. It provides you with a framework with which to carefully and deliberately interact with others in a way that strengthens the entire organization. At the end of the day, your personal success, the success of others, and the success of your organization all depend on one thing: people. *Leveraging Your Leadership Style* was written with you in mind…in order to give you a roadmap, a direction and confidence in the future so that you won't be like Supreme Court Justice Oliver Wendell Holmes. On one trip, apparently, Holmes had misplaced his ticket while traveling on a train. He searched for it, obviously irritated, as the conductor stood by waiting. Finally, the train official told Holmes, "Your Honor, if you do not find your ticket, you can simply mail it to the railroad. We know and trust you." Holmes replied, "I am not so concerned about your getting my ticket. I just want to know where I am going." [4]

You can be a "net investor" in the lives of the people you work with. When you understand the people that are on your team and maximize your relationship with them through proactive team building, you will be a better leader, build a better team, and leverage your leadership style!

> Effective executives never ask "How does he get along with me?" Their question is "What does he contribute?" Their question is never, "What can a man not do?" Their question is always "What can he do uncommonly well?" In staffing, they look for excellence in one major area, and not for performance that gets by all around.[5]

May we all honor the leadership style God has given us, take the time to invest in others, and leave a legacy behind, one we can be proud of. It is my great privilege to tell you that I believe in you! You are a special creation of God and He delights in seeing you become all that you can be—and your leadership of others will lead you to excellence way beyond "just getting by." Go leverage your leadership!

—**Dr. John Jackson**

You Don't Need a Title to Lead

As I (Lorraine) conclude this book, I'm reading the book called *You Don't Need a Title to Be a Leader* by my friend, Mark Sanborn. If you haven't read it yet, you must (youdontneedatitle.com). Mark has a way with words, challenging us through enlightening stories and illustrations. His message is spot on and really the essence of so much of what we have said through *Leveraging Your Leadership Style*—that anyone can be a leader—particularly if leadership is about influencing others. In fact, you are a leader whether you realize it or not. Someone, somewhere today has probably looked to you for guidance and direction. That makes you a leader! And based upon your specific personality, you show your leadership in different ways.

Looking back through my life, I was leading people at a very young age. It took years, though, to understand the scope of leadership, and as Mark says in his book, "leadership is a lifelong journey." One thing that should be a common factor for us all, though, is transforming lives and making a difference. What good are all of our experience and insight if we don't share it with others? As leaders, we must be deliberate, intentional, and persistent, no matter what our primary personality style.

Define Your Purpose

I'm a firm believer in personal mission statements. We are quite familiar with corporate mission statements at work. We live and die by them, actually. My question to you is this: Do you know why you were put on this earth? Certainly, it can't be to just "work." It goes deeper than that. Years ago now, I wrote my personal mission statement that communicates my purpose and existence, outside of what I do for a living. For men, this is even more critical since they have a tendency to "be what they do." Here is what I came up with:

I'm an encourager, a coach, if you will. My purpose is to help people succeed in whatever they do.

I open their eyes to the greatness that lies dormant within them.

I lead by example, and in doing so, inspire people to trust in themselves, pursue excellence, and reach beyond to their full potential.

I shall conquer what other men fear and dare not attempt.

I will be a light to the world, having a powerfully positive impact and influence.

I am a champion, an Ambassador for Christ.

I encourage you to draft something up for yourself and post it. What we do for a living really should be aligned with who we are and are asked to be. I bet you will see your leadership role shine through, no matter what your title is on the job. And it is your personal mission statement that helps you get out of bed every day. A job won't do that for you, but knowing God's purpose in your life will excite you and keep you charged up!

Have Goals

On a daily basis, I found myself wanting further focus to my mission, and I created what I call "G-O-A-L-S":

Grateful for all God has given me

Obedient to God's will and timing

Apply all I have learned or have been taught

Live life to the fullest and be financially stable doing so

Support all those I love and care about

This keeps everything simple, and I can take action. Too often we can make things more complicated than they should be. At work, systems are enhanced and improved when maybe the simplest method was the best. Technology was supposed to save us, but I fear the opposite is true. It has bogged our lives down. We are busy but not productive, and there is a difference! To me, it all boils down to taking action and doing what you know you should do. For the Commanders, this comes easier. They "fire then aim." Conductors get stuck at the "aim, aim, aim" stage, while Counselors may be "ready, ready, ready." Coaches can be all over the board with "aim, fire, ready!" We all have our strengths and weaknesses, but let us not get trapped by them. The difference between successful people and unsuccessful people is overcoming our challenges to take action.

"Courage is not the absence of fear;
rather it is the ability to take action in the face of fear."

—Nancy Anderson[6]

Live Life

Our world is full of examples of people who let us down and fail at the task at hand. Rather than concentrate on these, look to those who have lived a full life with purpose and intent. In the Disney movie, *Tuck Everlasting*, the dad, who was immortal, told his son, "Do not fear death but be afraid of an unlived life." Tragically, much of the world is sleepwalking and going through the motions of life. They need us; they need you! You have been given the gift of life along with skills and talents, like leadership. Our gift back to God should be using what He has given us, to the best of our ability. Maybe you, like me, don't feel that you were born a leader and that you had to really work at those skills—even more reason for you to use them for good, not gain. God developed you and had a purpose for it.

Our history books are filled with examples of fallen leaders who became power hungry and greedy. Controlling, manipulating, and forcing people to follow out of fear will lead to destruction, not to success. Some may experience short-term "highs," but they will not achieve long-term value and depth. This only comes from putting others first, which is what leadership is all about.

68

Leadership is a sacrifice—it is self-denial—it is love,
it is fearlessness, and it is humility, and it is in the perfectly disciplined will.
This is also the distinction between great and little people.
The harder you work, the harder it is to surrender.
The role of a leader is to enhance, transform, coach, care, trust, and cheerlead.
The activities of the leader are to educate, sponsor, coach, and counsel
using appropriate timing, tone, and consequences and skills.

—Tom Peters and Nancy Austin[7]

So go, Command, Coach, Counsel, and Conduct—and do it with style. Our blessings!

—Lorraine Bossé-Smith

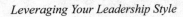

Book Notes

Chapter 1: The Lost Art of Leadership

1. Rick Warren, *The Purpose Driven Life* (Grand Rapids, Mich.: Zondervan Publishing, 2002), 17.

2. Robert Harold Schuller, *Your Church Has Real Possibilities* (Glendale, Calif.: G/L Regal Books, 1974), 4.

3. Frances Hesselbein, Marshall Goldsmith, and Richard Beckhard, eds., *The Leader of the Future: New Visions, Strategies, and Practices for the Next Era* (San Francisco: Jossey-Bass, 1996), xii.

4. John C. Maxwell, *Developing the Leader Within You* (Nashville: Thomas Nelson, 1993), 1.

Chapter 2: Identifying Your Leadership Style

1. Marita Littauer and Florence Littauer, *Wired That Way* (Ventura, Calif.: Regal Books, 2006), 13.

2. Ibid., 14.

Chapter 3: Understanding Your Leadership Style

1. W. Steven Brown quoted in Glenn Van Ekeren, *The Speaker's Sourcebook II* (Englewood Cliffs, NJ: Prentice Hall, 1994), 71.

Chapter 4: The Commander

1. Maxwell, *Developing the Leader Within You*, 172.

2. "Management by Walking Away," Web. 1 October 1983, Inc.com/magazine/19831001/5444.html. Also cited in Thomas J. Peters and Nancy Austin, *A Passion for Excellence* (New York: Warner Books, 1985), 256.

3. John Jackson, *PastorPreneur* (Carson City, Nev.: VisionQuest Ministries, 2003), 3.

4. Andy Stanley, *Next Generation Leader: 5 Essentials for Those Who Will Shape the Future* (Sisters, Ore.: Multnomah Publishers, 2003), 55.

5. Rick Warren cited by Maxwell, *Developing the Leader Within You*, 144.

6. "James Crook Quotes," Web. 17 May 2015, goodreads.com/author/quotes/4277333. James_Crook.

7. J. Oswald Sanders, *Spiritual Leadership: A Commitment to Excellence for Every Believer* (Commitment to Spiritual Growth) revised ed., (Chicago: Moody Press, 1994), 76.

Chapter 5: The Coach

1. Chuck and Barbara Snyder, *Incompatibility: Grounds for a Great Marriage* (Sisters, Ore.: Multnomah Publishers, 1999), 22.

2. Buck Roger quoted in Van Ekeren, *The Speaker's Sourcebook II,* 224.

Chapter 6: The Counselor

1. John C. Maxwell, *The Success Journey* (Nashville: Thomas Nelson, 1997), 11.

2. "Things Leaders Do: GE's Jeff Immelt, on the 10 Keys to Great Leadership," *Fast Company,* April 2004, 96.

Chapter 7: The Conductor

1. Stephen R. Covey, *The 7 Habits of Highly Effective People* (New York: Free Press, 2004) 220.

2. "That Was Funny: Where all jokes are safe for work," Web. 17 May 2015, thatwasfunny.com/2006/12/16/new-company-policies/857/.

3. Gail Sheehy cited in Van Ekeren, *The Speaker's Sourcebook II*, 179.

Chapter 8: Model Team Leadership with Style

1. Peter F. Drucker, *The Effective Executive*, revised ed. (New York: HarperCollins, 2002), 23-24.

2. *Rev! Magazine,* June 2006. See also Pastorpreneur.com and the link to John Jackson's leadership blog on that same site.

3. John C. Maxwell, *Leadership Wired* 6 no. 20 (December 2003) 1.

4. Thomas Ranier, "Leaders Admit Top 5 Weaknesses," Web. November 2004, churchcentral.com/news/leaders-admit-top-5-weaknesses/.

5. Covey, *The 7 Habits of Highly Effective People*, 287.

6. Richard S. Wellins quoted in William M. Easum, *Sacred Cows Make Gourmet Burgers: Ministry Anytime, Anywhere, by Anyone* (Nashville: Abingdon Press, 1995), 113.

Conclusion: Leveraging Your Leadership Style!

1. John Godfrey Saxe, "The Blind Men and the Elephant," Web. 17 May 2015, PoemHunter.com/poem/the-blind-man-and-the-elephant/.

2. Robert K. Cooper, *The Other 90%: How to Unlock Your Vast Untapped Potential for Leadership and Life* (New York: Three Rivers Press, 2001), 251.

3. Carol Clark cited by Virginia Galt, *The Globe and Mail*, 11 April 2003.

4. Maxwell, *The Success Journey,* 76.

5. Drucker, *The Effective Executive*, revised ed., 74.

6. Nancy Anderson quoted in Van Ekeren, *The Speaker's Sourcebook II*, 76.

7. Thomas J. Peters and Nancy Austin quoted in Van Ekeren, *The Speaker's Sourcebook II*, 224.

Bibliography

All references to the Bible are the New International Translation (NIV).

Bakke, Dennis. *Joy at Work*. Seattle, WA: PVG, 2005.

Cooper, Robert. *The Other 90%: How to Unlock Your Vast Untapped Potential for Leadership and Life*. New York, NY: Three Rivers Press, 2001.

Covey, Stephen R. *The 7 Habits of Highly Effective People*. New York, NY: Free Press, 2004.

Dooley, Ken. *Good Staff*. Malvern, PA: Progressive Business Publishing, 2004.

Drucker, Peter. *The Effective Executive,* revised ed. New York, NY: Harper-Collins, 1993.

Easum, William. *Sacred Cows Make Gourmet Burgers*. Nashville, TN: Abingdon Press, 1995.

Farrar, Steve. *Finishing Strong*. Sisters, OR: Multnomah Publishers, 2002.

Galt, Virginia. *The Globe and Mail*, 11 April, 2003.

Haughton, Laurence. *It's Not What You Say, It's What You Do*. New York, NY: Currency Publishers, 2004.

Hesselbein, Frances and Paul Cohen, eds. *Leader to Leader*. San Francisco, CA: Jossey-Bass, 1999.

Jackson, John. *PastorPreneur*. Carson City, NV: VisionQuest Ministries, 2003.

"James Crook Quotes." Web. 17 May, 2015. goodreads.com/author/quotes/ 4277333.james_crook.

Kouzes, Jim and Barry Posner. *The Leadership Challenge*. San Francisco, CA: Jossey-Bass, 2002

Lencioni, Patrick. *The Five Dysfunctions of a Team*. San Francisco, CA: Jossey-Bass, 2002.

Littauer, Marita. *Wired That Way*. Ventura, Calif.: Regal Books, 2006.

——. *You've Got What It Takes*. Minneapolis, MN: Bethany House Publishers, 2000.

"Management by Walking Away." Web. 1 October 1983. Inc.com/magazine/19831001/5444.html.

Maxwell , John C. *21 Irrefutable Laws of Leadership*. Nashville, TN: Thomas Nelson Publishing, 1998.

——. *The 360° Leader*. Nashville, TN: Thomas Nelson Publishing, 2006.

——. *Developing The Leader Within You*. Nashville: Thomas Nelson, Inc. 1993

——. *Leadership Wired Blog* 6 no. 20. December 2003.

Peters, Thomas J. and Nancy Austin. *A Passion for Excellence: The Leadership Difference*. New York: Warner Books, 1985.

Ranier, Thomas. "Leaders Admit Top 5 Weaknesses." Web. November 2004. churchcentral.com/news/leaders-admit-top-5-weaknesses/.

Rev! Magazine. June 2006.

Rohm, Robert, *Positive Personality Profiles*. Atlanta, GA: Personality Insights, 2003.

Sanders, J. Oswald. *Spiritual Leadership,* revised ed. Chicago, IL: Moody Publishers, 1994.

Saxe, John Godfrey. "The Blind Men and the Elephant." Web. 17 May 2015. PoemHunter.com/poem/the-blind-man-and-the-elephant/.

Senge, Peter. *The Fifth Discipline*. New York, NY: Currency Publishers, 1990.

Stanley, Andy. *The Next Generation Leader*. Sisters, OR: Multnomah Publishers, 2003.

Snyder, Chuck and Barbara. *Incompatibility: Grounds for a Great Marriage*. Sisters, OR: Multnomah Publishers, 1999.

"That Was Funny: Where all jokes are safe for work," Web. 17 May 2015. thatwasfunny.com/2006/12/16/new-company-policies/857/.

Van Ekeren, Glenn. *The Speaker's Sourcebook II*. Englewood Cliffs, NJ: Prentice Hall, Inc., 1994.

Warren, Rick. *The Purpose Driven Life*. Grand Rapids, MI: Zondervan Publishing, 2002.

Leveraging Your Leadership Style Workbook

John Jackson and Lorraine Bossé-Smith

Jessup University Press

INTRODUCTION
Transform Your Leadership

Ready to take a road trip? I'm assuming by now that you have read the book, *Leveraging Your Leadership Style,* and now you want to take some more practical steps to equip yourself and team members. In some of the chapters that I (John) write, I'll be using the analogy of a road trip. I grew up in a family that took LONG road trips (counted in days, not miles!). I knew the privilege and the pain of taking a road trip with a family full of different kinds of travelers...every one of which is now a different kind of leader. I complained the entire length of the trips, but when I arrived at adulthood, those road trips were some of my fondest memories (thanks Dad & Mom!).

You have taken your own road trips in the course of your life. Whether or not these trips have been in a car or in a variety of different life experiences in corporate and personal situations, you have learned about leadership on your journey. You may not think of yourself as a leader, but the truth is that you are. In fact, here is what I know: You actually know more about leadership than you think you know. Our definition of leadership is "leveraging influence in the context of healthy relationships," and you have been exercising leadership whether you know it or not!

You are a person of influence and a leader. You influence others and want to be more effective with your leadership and your relationships. You'll get the most help from this workbook if you go slowly. I know that many of you are "Type A" driven leaders (Welcome...We are too!), and you'll want to speed through the exercises. Resist the urge! Yes I know...I'm probably risking your emotional equilibrium, but I believe you can do it. Instead of hydroplaning over the surface of the material, take your time to absorb it...and then share your conclusions with your key team members. Work the materials into the context of your teambuilding time rather than just "doing" the materials as an assignment.

The goal of this workbook is to give you very practical tools so that you can be a better leader and equip your team to be a better team. Commanders, you will finish this workbook (probably first!). Coaches, you can enjoy these pages with your team, and you'll make it fun! Counselors, you will be enriched by the process, and you can add value to each of your team members through the process. Conductors, you will be efficient and effective throughout the process, and you will cross the finish line! So, fasten your seatbelt and start your engines…we're ready to roll!

—**Dr. John Jackson**

The movie *Transformers* is a live-action (computer-enhanced, of course) version of a decades-old cartoon in which semi-tractor-trailer trucks and other vehicles change and become something even more powerful. The movie introduces us to good and evil transformers, all with their own objectives. I believe the same is true of leaders: inside each of us, we have something great waiting to explode! In every one of us is also the ability to do good or bad with what we have inside. All one needs to do is read the paper or watch the news to discover plenty of folks in both camps. Our history books are full of amazing leaders who founded the very country we live in today. On the same pages are corrupt and misguided leaders who have attempted to destroy society as we know it.

Leveraging Your Leadership Style and this companion workbook are not books of psychology but rather insights into the behaviors or personality temperaments that we all have been given. What we do with them is our choice, and I'm very glad that you have decided to put your gifts and talents to good use! As leaders, no matter what our role or title, we have a responsibility to others. And great leadership starts within.

Just like the *Transformers* toys or characters from the movie, we must control what comes out to the public. We all have strengths that, when pushed to an extreme, can become weaknesses or negative traits. The more we know about ourselves, the better we can lead. Couple this with a ferocious appetite to understand others, and you have the makings of a remarkable leader…one that people follow because of who you are, not because of your position.

I truly believe that any person in leadership desires such a healthy leader-follower relationship deep down inside. Some may have forgotten why they got into leadership, falling prey to worldly/trendy/false views. Others may doubt that such a bond can be formed. Have hope! Building bridges and creating stronger teams is what leveraging your leadership style is all about. And with this workbook, you will learn how to apply the strategies discussed in specific situations. Consider this practice, and practice makes perfect.

How do professional tennis players get on the circuit? By playing tennis…a lot! They didn't just show up one day. Instead, they hit a bazillion tennis balls behind the scenes. By the time you and I see them on television, they are experts. You have been exposed to some new ideas on leadership and how your particular style influences others. Now it is your turn to hit a few balls, practice your serve and get in the game of leading with style.

You will need a copy of *Leveraging Your Leadership Style* and will want to take the assessment. I highly encourage you to read through the chapter that corresponds to your particular style before diving into the workbook. This workbook will compliment what you have learned and take it to the next level by providing you with very realistic case studies. You will have the opportunity to think and determine how you would respond to these hypothetical dilemmas, all in the safety of this book. This isn't about winning and conquering your opponent, though—it is about becoming a better leader, one to be proud of in years to come.

—Lorraine Bossé-Smith

CHAPTER ONE

Building Bridges

L everaging your leadership style is all about positive and proactive influence in the context of healthy relationships. What that means in practical terms is that leaders have to learn to operate using their own leadership style in relationship (and sometimes in tension!) with everyone else on their team. Marcus Buckingham, author of *First Break All the Rules*, suggests that leaders need to understand several different aspects of those they work with:

Striving Talents, Thinking Talents, and Relating Talents

> **Striving** talents explain the *why* of a person. They explain *why* we get out of bed every day, why we are motivated to push, and push just that little bit harder.

> **Thinking** talents explain the *how* of a person. They explain *how* we think, *how* we weigh alternatives, *how* we come to decisions.

> **Relating** talents explain the *who* of a person. They explain *whom* we trust, *whom* we build relationships with, *whom* he confronts and whom he ignores.[1]

As you think about the striving, thinking, and relating talents of each of your team members, you will no doubt begin to reference our four leadership styles: Commander, Coach, Counselor, and Conductor. Each of the leadership styles has a different approach to being on the team and leading the team. For you as a team leader or team participant, your challenge is to understand the "why," the "how," and the "who" of people's participation and leadership within a team environment. The more you can understand yourself and others as well as the interaction between them, the more you'll leverage your leadership! This workbook will help you to put into real-life practice the principles we described in the *Leveraging Your Leadership Style* book itself.

A Trip Down Memory Lane

When I (John) was a kid, my parents never liked owning a home. In fact, they have only ever owned one home. It had a pool and was really nice. But, it took a lot of work, and it kept them from the one thing they loved for us to do together… travel! I can't tell you how many "road trips" we took when I was a kid. In fact, one of the luxuries of my dad's 24/7 job was that we got 3 to 4 weeks of vacation every year. So as a kid, I learned to count vacations not in light of miles traveled, but in days gone from home! I complained terribly (mostly about riding in a cramped backseat with my three siblings), but as an adult, those trip memories are some of my greatest childhood treasures.

So, I thought we'd take a short road trip together. I've become convinced that every team and every leader are a little bit like drivers and passengers on the road trips of my childhood. In fact, each trip is different based on what the driver is like. Think about the teams you serve on or perhaps the teams you lead. Do any of these road trip descriptions sound familiar to you?

Road Trip!

Road Trips with a Commander: Commanders are about achieving the goal. Finishing the journey is the most important thing. Well, not exactly. Finishing the trip is close to being the *only* thing! Getting there ahead of schedule, ahead of others and ahead of projected personal calculations are the primary objectives. If you are a passenger with a Commander, do not drink any water. Bathroom stops are highly discouraged! Side trips will only happen for this group if they are a short cut! A passenger traveling with a Commander driver will finish the journey before anyone else. But, unless this group is full of Commanders, it is probably not the happiest carload of people.

Road Trips with a Coach: Coaches are about the team. Making sure that all the passengers in the vehicle are happy with each other is a key concern. Coaches develop a game plan that will help them complete the journey, but they are also very concerned that the team members are fulfilled on the journey. If you are a passenger with a Coach, be prepared for frequent rest stops to make sure everyone is "on-board." In fact, a side trip might even happen if **everyone** agrees that it would be fun. Passengers traveling with good Coach drivers will finish the journey—**together**.

Road Trips with a Counselor: Counselors are about the health of the individual. Counselors want to know that each person is fulfilled, living a life of purpose and meaning, and also fulfilling their potential. Taking a road trip with a Counselor? Expect frequent probing, supportive, and penetrating questions about how you are experiencing the journey. Side trips for this group could happen if the driver is convinced that it would be personally enriching to each passenger. You will probably arrive at your destination later than most, but you will have a great deal more understanding of the journey you've traveled.

Road Trips with a Conductor: Conductors are about the strategy and the structure of the trip. Conductors will want to ensure that the trip is well planned, researched, and executed. Mileage markers (and bathroom stops!) will be known in advance and calculated. Conductors will start later than others because of the preparation time involved, but the overall efficiency of the trip should far surpass any other driving type; and if it doesn't, expect pressure! Passengers traveling with Conductors can rightly expect an on-time arrival with the most direct route planned in advance. Don't expect time for side trips on this bus; they don't fit into the efficient schedule the Conductor has planned.

So, have you taken a road trip with one of these drivers? Have you *been* one of these drivers? I hope you are smiling…because I bet you recognize yourself in these drivers. I know I do (and I'm sure my poor family recognizes me as well!). Self-awareness is a key to leadership.

Let's Hit the Road

Growing and developing your work teams is a little bit like taking a road trip. Sometimes we can get cranky with our fellow passengers under ordinary circumstances; and if your team members have widely different styles, your road trip may feel more like crossing the plains in a covered wagon! You'll have to think through what kind of driver you are and what kind of passengers you have in your car. Spend a moment now and think that one through.

1. What kind of driver are you on a road trip? What is the highest value for you when you are taking a long journey?

_____

_____

_____

2. Pretend you are taking your family of four on a 500-mile road trip in your family car. How would you go about preparing for the trip? What would the trip be like for your passengers?

_____

_____

_____

3. Think for a moment about your team. Do they think just like you? Or, are you often surprised (annoyed?) when they appear to have different values or priorities than you? See if you can identify what type of driver each member of your primary team would be if they were taking a road trip.

_____

_____

_____

Making the Trip Together

In our history books, the true heroes and exceptional leaders did not make decisions from an ivory tower. Rather, they were in the trenches, alongside their troops. Consider giving your team this road trip exercise during a staff meeting or corporate retreat. Have everyone think about the above questions and then share what his or her potential road trip was like. Better yet, break the ice by having your team bring in and share a photo of their favorite road trip! Just as my family trips (and subsequent trips as an adult) taught me a great deal about others and myself, this exercise can really shed some light (and laughter) on your team.

As a leader, I encourage you to take time for some short road trips for your team—especially your top management or executive staff. The more time you spend together, the stronger the bridge will be between you. Now that is leveraging your leadership style!

CHAPTER TWO
Create Stronger Relationships

I hope you enjoyed John's road trip analogy in chapter one! For those who are fast-paced, you may want to skip right to the chapter focusing on your particular leadership style. However, if you are interested in understanding why it is so critical for you and your business to build stronger relationships, we invite you to join us for this chapter. Those who appreciate facts and statistics will definitely want to absorb this information. Research offers many insights into the value of relationships in organizations and what needs to be done in order to grow businesses beyond today.

We already know that leadership is all about relationships. And according to the American Management Association, the future of business depends upon them.[1] With the aging of the population and a new breed of workers, businesses must respond correctly, or we all could be in a world of hurt. Down to an inter-personal level, leaders need to pay attention to the changes in the marketplace in order to make necessary adaptations.

Job dissatisfaction is at an all-time high. AMA reports that only 29 percent of workers feel engaged on the job. Workers are no longer staying put and suffering through a poor work environment.[2] Mark Sanborn, author of the best-selling book, *The Fred Factor*, states that the number one reason why employees leave is a lack of appreciation.[3] Couple that with an upcoming shortage of people able to work (due to the retirement of baby boomers), and we better pay attention and get more serious about the relationships we have with our employees.

I recently heard a story of a man who called an emergency meeting with his management staff to do something about the company's high turnover. He proposed that new incentives and benefits be introduced to entice employees to stay. A brave executive addressed the president and asked, "Sir, have you ever considered that we might be part of the problem?" You may have heard it said before: "People don't leave jobs; they leave bosses." Ouch! Although it can sting, as leaders we need to acknowledge and accept responsibility. The way we communicate, direct, coach, counsel, and conduct ourselves does impact the entire organization. If things aren't going as we would like, we need to look inward first before blaming processes. Certainly, all systems can be evaluated and possibly improved, but sometimes the problem lies within.

We're Not in Kansas Anymore!

The 2000 Bureau of Labor Statistics estimated that by the year 2008 our country would have 5 to 6.2 million more jobs than people able to fill them, and they were right! Businesses are already feeling the crunch, having difficulty recruiting and retaining top talent.[4] As leaders, we have to create stronger relationships and engage employees—money only goes so far as a motivator. Work environment is essential. Judith Glaser, author of *Creating WE: Change I-Thinking to We-Thinking & Build a Healthy, Thriving Organization*, points out that people want a place to develop and flourish.[5] Employees want to be valued for their contributions and recognized for meeting those audacious goals management can set. In short, they want to be allowed to succeed. As leaders, we must provide that atmosphere. How? By knowing what people want.

Every one of your employees and customers has a unique set of issues and needs for you to consider. Caring enough to *know* your people will reduce your turnover and increase job satisfaction. By motivating, managing, encouraging, and rewarding people based upon their unique preferences, you will save yourself a lot of heartache…and money.

The president of a company I worked for many years ago impressed me so much that I still remember it. He had run the company for twenty-five plus years. We were at a trade show specific to our industry, and as he walked the floor, he greeted each and every person by his or her first name. This alone was amazing, given that he was greeting hundreds of people, but what really got me was how he remembered what was going on in their lives. He'd ask how their son was doing in college or if they recovered from the surgery they had last year. He truly took an interest in his customers, and had a gift for retaining the details of their lives—a gift that we don't all have. However, we can all get to know the people on our team intimately.

> *"People don't care about how much you know until they know how much you care."*
>
> –Anonymous

Bobby Bowden, head football coach for the Florida State Seminoles, lists compassion right alongside integrity and courage as key virtues of great leaders. According to Bowden, it is critical to not only be honest with your people and stand up for what you believe in but to have a deep love for those working under you.[6]

I (Lorraine) have worked for numerous nonprofit organizations in my corporate career. Salaries are typically lower and the workload heavier than in other jobs. Yet, as a leader, I was able to build strong teams of employees who were satisfied and engaged. What I couldn't give them in monetary rewards I gave them in encouragement, support, and career enhancement. Never underestimate what training or a seminar can do for an employee. Besides improving their job skills, personnel often feel valued and appreciated. The underlying message they hear is clear: "They wouldn't invest in a deadbeat employee…I must matter."

Make a Difference

I believe everyone wants to matter and to make a difference, regardless of his or her position. I also think the aging of our country's employees is going to force everyone to lead better and be more creative with how they motivate, reward, and retain top talent. That's a good thing! Throwing money at problems never really solves them—it just hides them or delays the inevitable. As leaders, we must throw ourselves in, role up our sleeves, and get relational.

Getting Serious

OK, so maybe you haven't done an exceptional job of building up your team up until now. If so, start today. John Maxwell, leadership guru, reminds us that yesterday ended last night. He encourages us not to "over exaggerate yesterday or underestimate today because the one thing we have is today."[7] We can't change our past decisions, but we can learn from them. What is incredible about doing the right things from this point forward is that you will dramatically change tomorrow. The future success of your business will be influenced by what you do today. Think for a moment about these questions:

1. How well do you know your employees?

_____

_____

_____

2. What could you do to get to know them better and to show your interest in their lives?

_____

_____

_____

3. Besides money, how could you show your employees that they matter to you?

_____

_____

_____

> *"If people are coming to work excited...*
> *if they're making mistakes freely and fearlessly...*
> *if they're having fun...*
> *if they're concentrating on doing things*
> *rather than preparing reports and going to meetings—*
> *then somewhere, you have a leader."*
>
> –Robert Townsend[8]

Begin looking at your employees as associates or partners. They aren't showing up to serve you but rather to work alongside of you to achieve a common goal. If you have done your job right, you have cast the vision. And this vision is what brings them back day after day. The more you invest in them and challenge them to reach their full potential, the more engaged they will become. The scary part of AMA's recent report is that not only are workers not engaged, 15 percent of them are totally disengaged. We have work to do![9]

In *Leveraging Your Leadership Style*, John and I talk about mentoring. AMA is also finding that companies who offer a mentoring program are retaining employees at higher percentages.[10] As employees build relationships with their mentors, they feel more connected to the company on a personal level. Mentoring is all about leading through relationships. Are you seeing the trend here? We are at a crossroads; what we've done in the past isn't going to work in the future…not if we want to achieve greatness. We cannot look at employees as projects or costs in our business, rather, they are the business.

> *"We are not primarily put on this earth to see through one another,*
> *but to see one another through."*
>
> –Peter DeVries[11]

Take advantage of this workbook and learn as much about the different personalities as you can. Work on adapting your style so you can reach more people with ease. Here we go!

CHAPTER THREE

Commanders Get'er Done!

Enough said, right? As Commanders, you naturally want to get results, achieve goals, and do it all fast. Commanders work at the speed of light, but not everyone else in the world can keep up, thus you can feel frustrated at times with your less-efficient colleagues. I know you are good at whatever you do, but this chapter will help you do it even better. Bottom line, it will help you be more successful by adapting slightly to influence others.

By now, you understand the different leadership/personality styles. Now I (Lorraine) will offer some real situations and see if you have captured the essence of approaching people differently. You're a person on the go, so let's jump right in.

Case Study #1: Budget Blues

You have just received news that budgets must be cut. Everyone just burned the midnight oil to get their numbers turned in, and now they must revise them—most likely having to cut in places where it will hurt. Company goals and objectives remain. On your team, you have a customer service manager who is very supportive of her team and often petitions their feedback before she makes decisions. You also have a very outgoing, positive sales manager who really struggled with the budget because he is more comfortable with relationships than numbers. Your marketing manager is a high achiever who is aggressive and pushes her team hard. Your controller—a very analytical number cruncher—has been instrumental in the process, but nonetheless, he will also be required to slash his budget.

1. Without demoralizing everyone, how do you communicate to the group the change in plans and the need for new numbers?

_____

_____

_____

2. How would you specifically address your customer service manager?

_____

_____

_____

3. Your sales manager?

_____

_____

_____

4. Your marketing manager?

_____

_____

_____

5. Your controller?

_____

_____

_____

The Opportunities

So, did you meet one-on-one or gather the group together for a debrief? Both have pros and cons. You'll save time getting everyone together at once, but you may lose the opportunity to specifically target your news to each manager. If you don't already have them, I would encourage you to have weekly one-on-ones with your management team. They don't have to be long, but you can keep on top of things and speak directly to their particular leadership style, which will get you further ahead in the long run.

Your customer service manager is most likely a Counselor. She will be distressed over how her team will be affected by the budget. You will want to address her concerns for her people, which will mean actually slowing down long enough to *hear* her concerns. Encourage her to get her team involved so that it isn't a shock to them. Help her look on the bright side: that the team can pull together on this.

Your sales manager is probably a Coach and will feel overwhelmed if you provide too many details, so keep it simple and to the point, yet don't box him in. Allow creativity here and focus on the end goal, not how he gets there. This will relieve some of the pressure so that he doesn't get "stuck."

Your marketing manager, who is a Commander, will be difficult to slow down enough to discuss the budget, and she probably won't be happy about having to spend more time on it. Emphasize any bonuses associated with working within the new budget parameters and create some challenges for her—doing more with less! If you can tap into her competitive spirit, that will be even better.

Your controller, a Conductor, will want to know specifics. Give your feedback as to what you think should be done in a concise manner and be clear with the deadline without being too forceful. Your controller should be comfortable in this arena.

Case Study #2: Client Case

A major client contacted you directly about his frustration with your company. He came to you first before deciding to take his business elsewhere. In the conversation, you learned that delivery dates had been promised by the sales department but were not met. In addition, he had to call personally for the status update, which means customer service was not proactive. Accounting sent him the bill for a shipment he hadn't even received, and no one in production has returned his call to date.

Your sales manager is a Commander, your customer service manager is a Coach, your accounting manager is a Counselor, and your production manager is a Conductor. When you bring the management team together to discuss this important client, everyone starts pointing fingers and stating, "Well he said," "She was supposed to," etc.

1. What do you focus on in the meeting? How do you communicate in such a manner that works for every member of the team without losing the urgency of the situation?

2. What action do you expect of your sales manager, and how do you express it?

_____

_____

_____

3. Of your customer service manager?

_____

_____

_____

4. Of your accounting manager?

_____

_____

_____

5. Of your production manager?

_____

_____

_____

The Solutions

Obviously, you need to make things right for your client. You must first get to the bottom of the situation and learn what really happened. As the leader, your job is to discover what went wrong without assigning blame. Provide an environment that is direct, encouraging, safe, and specific in order to keep each of your managers engaged. When you do, you'll get honesty, not responsibility-dodging.

As you interact with your sales manager, a Commander, be sure to commend his high-energy sales efforts but reinforce the objective, which is ultimately client satisfaction. Stress the goal and ask him how he intends to do things different in the future to avoid such a situation again.

Your customer service manager, a Coach, will need to know how upset your client really is, and how the relationship has suffered as a result but is not beyond repair. Compliment her on her ability to create rapport with people and encourage her to make things right with the customer. Suggest that she assess all customer relations at the present and perhaps beef up contact in order to increase satisfaction levels, which will make her job easier and more enjoyable.

Your accounting manager, a Counselor, will feel horrible about the error. Turn his energy away from guilt to "how to remedy the situation." Ask some active questions to draw him into a positive solution that he will be eager to implement and to make standard policy for future dealings. Just remember to allow him to speak, which may require a silence on your part. Drink some water while you wait!

Last, your product manager, a Conductor, has most likely gotten paralyzed by analysis and is stuck in the numbers or systems of the business. She hasn't lifted her head up to see what is really transpiring around her. Encourage her to meet with her team and get facts and figures on how they are performing, or not performing. Give her a deadline to present you with a solution/system/procedure that will correct this broken link in the chain. Don't push too hard at the initial meeting to get answers. Allow her time to gather her thoughts and get back to you. Then, give her the floor to present her ideas to you at the appropriate time and ask intelligent questions that will help guide her to the right conclusion.

Real Life

In these cases, as it is with life, many more variables exist; but you get the idea that *how* you approach people and situations can set them up for success. Rather than fighting over the words, you are moving ahead to solutions—faster and more effectively!

> *"Everything that irritates us about others*
> *can lead to an understanding of ourselves."*
>
> –Carl Jung[1]

CHAPTER FOUR
Coaches Make It Fun!

As Coaches, you bring an element of fun wherever you go. Unfortunately, certain aspects of leadership can be difficult, but that doesn't mean it has to be impossible or total drudgery. You are a master at building rapport with people. Couple your natural talents with the understanding you have gained of the different personalities, and you have a recipe for very exciting times! This chapter will help you be more engaging with others and create better teams by adapting your style to influence others.

Observe any team, and you will see every style. The very best television programs use the synergy between the blends. Look at *Seinfeld*: Kramer's high energy is fun and contagious, like you Coaches. Elaine's opinions, strong will, and determination are admirable, like the Commanders. Jerry is always supporting everyone and trying to keep the peace, like Counselors, while George has systems, schedules, and structures for just about everything—even dating (what a Conductor)! The show wouldn't be as lively without the combination of all personalities. It is what makes the show.

As a Coach, you might wish that everyone would lighten up a bit, but sometimes the best approach is what works for someone else. I (Lorraine) am going to offer some real situations for you that provide the opportunity to alter your interactions to fit others. Use what you have learned so far and make it fun.

Case Study #1: Breaking Up Is Hard to Do

You are the president of a large ministry organization/nonprofit. You inherited a fellow who is steamrolling over those below him and pushing the buttons of those above him. He is abrasive, controlling, and not living out the mission statement in his role as director. After jumping through all the hoops, crossing your t's and dotting your i's, you come to the conclusion that you must let him go. And by the way, he's the founder's brother-in-law.

1. How do you handle the situation with the founder, who is a Conductor?

_____

_____

_____

2. How do you conduct the exit interview with the director?

_____

_____

_____

3. How do you break the news to the director's secretary, who is a Counselor?

_____

_____

_____

4. The director's fund-raising team consists of three Coaches. How do you communicate the news to them without jeopardizing financial goals?

_____

_____

_____

The Scoop

"Jumping through the hoops" means that you obtained approval for this very delicate matter. But, you must still handle the founder with "kid gloves." Facts are facts. They aren't subjective but objective. Diligently gather documentation and notes in your file, along with anything from human resources that they have, and confidently present the situation and why you resolved it the way you did. Remember, the director was hurting the ministry/nonprofit and not adhering to the mission statement. Point out these disregards for policies and procedures as well as the human impact to the founder. He is a man of logic, so as long as you have a solid case, you *should* be fine.

Any matter of this nature can be sticky, but when you communicate in a manner that matches the person's style, you won't add additional sparks to the already hot topic. I know this can be unpleasant and draining for you, but by adapting yourself to the founder, you will ultimately create a friendly environment.

As far as the director goes, you will need to prepare yourself for the attack. If he has blatantly broken rules and steamrolled over people, he will attempt to do the same to you. Chances are, he will be very direct and abrupt. In his mind, he is always right and did nothing wrong. First, I'd encourage you to have a witness— probably someone from HR. Second, do not try to fight with him; you won't stand a chance. Instead, take charge by hitting the bottom line without all the details. Although you might feel better listing all the mistakes he has made, it will only make him hotter. Be direct, firm, to the point, and remember to stick to business all the way. Control your emotions.

Set a time to conduct the exit interview and conclude it on your timetable. Provide the director an opportunity to gather his things. Do try to allow him the dignity of walking out on his own. However, if he gets out of control, then you will need to have security escort him off the premises. Keep in mind at all times, he is still the founder's brother in-law even if he isn't an employee anymore. Be respectful.

You will need to notify his secretary prior to the exit interview. Again, this is another sticky situation. She will feel loyalty to her boss. She must keep this in confidence. The best scenario is to have someone break the news to her while you are conducting the exit interview. Whoever tells her must show compassion for the awkwardness and communicate some plan so that she knows what to expect tomorrow. Change without all the supporting personal details is difficult for Counselors to swallow. You cannot go into details with her, but you can assure her of future security. Focus on how she can rebuild a steady, safe environment sooner rather than later, and she will handle the transition better.

When you address the director's team, be positive about what they have accomplished together and even praise individuals, if you can, for their efforts. Remind the team that they are talented, gifted, and good at what they do. Be sure to communicate what you know about *who* they will be reporting to, as this is critical to them. Even if you have a temporary arrangement, let them know so that they can focus their energies on doing their jobs rather than wondering who they will be working with.

Intensely negative situations like this one are never fun, but Coaches can have confidence in the fact that extracting the source of negativity to a team will improve the group's experience and effectiveness overall. It is important to realize that even those things that are flat-out painful can be done in a more pleasant way when we use the principles outlined in *Leveraging Your Leadership Style*.

"The task ahead of us is never as great as the Power behind us."

–Anonymous[1]

Case Study #2: Trade Off

The project manager for your company's industry trade show just quit, leaving behind many unfinished details such as confirmation of booth specs and requirements, product and service features, marketing and publicity, sales appointments, and travel arrangements. You were a part of the team but have now been promoted to acting project manager because of your rapport with everyone. You are an encourager but have been tasked with ensuring a successful event. Your team consists of a Commander, Coach, Counselor, and Conductor. You have a month to pull it all together.

1. What is the Commander's strength, what should you delegate to her, and how should you communicate it to her?

_____

_____

_____

2. What is the Coach's strength, what should you delegate to him, and how should you communicate it to him?

_____

_____

_____

3. What is the Counselor's strength, what should you delegate to him, and how should you communicate it to him?

_____

_____

_____

4. What is the Conductor's strength, what should you delegate to her, and how should you communicate it to her?

_____

_____

_____

T-E-A-M

You might feel uncomfortable at first delegating to your peers, but keep in mind that you will all be working as a team. Everyone just needs to pull together to make the trade show happen. And since you all get along, you can have some fun in the process! Communicating it right from the beginning will be the key.

As you assess the workload, look for the difficult challenges that your Commander can go after for you. She will have no difficulty contacting the media at the last minute to arrange some promotion, for instance. The pressure of being behind might actually force her to perform even better. Provide a priority list and let her go! How she does it, is up to her.

Consider your fellow Coach for any relationship-oriented aspects of the show such as contacting accounts and arranging sales calls. He will probably have the best relationships, other than you, of anyone on the team and will enjoy the opportunity of talking with people and possibly meeting them at the show. Compliment him on his ability to relate with people and emphasize how important the relationships are to the success of the show, and he will make things happen in a New York minute!

Your Counselor member would be a good fit for something a bit more behind the scenes yet still critical, such as the travel arrangements. He can work on this on his timetable but will have sensitivity to everyone's needs and requests. He might feel under pressure simply because of the urgency of the show, but if you offer some support and proper tools (like the travel budget and the name of the agency the company uses), he will be happy to help.

Conductors love details, so anything that requires streams of paperwork, precision, calculations, and measurements is ideal for them. Your Conductor would be best suited for the booth specs and any unique requirements you have for the show: power plugs, lighting, A/V, and so forth. Be sure to give her the exact deadlines that everything must be done and encourage her to seek help if she gets stuck.

A big event like this will have an array of activities, but with attention to each person's leadership style, you can divvy up the jobs to match everyone's strengths. You can also see that how you delegate it can make a world of difference. Everyone can do what they are best at and have fun!

Real Life

In these cases, as it is with life, many more variables exist, but how you approach people and situations can set them up for success. Rather than dodging responsibility or playing the blame game, you are focusing on the heart of the matter and enjoying the process a bit more.

> *"The will of God never takes you to where*
> *the Grace of God will not protect you."*
>
> –Anonymous

CHAPTER FIVE
Counselors Know Why It Matters

Personally, I thank God for all Counselors. You are others-focused by design, team-oriented naturally, and truly invest in relationships as a way of life. The teams you build tend to be very close and loyal. Your care and concern for others, however, can get in the way when it comes to leadership. The difficult, messy, and stressful aspects of being in charge can be a struggle for you. Thankfully, you have learned that it doesn't mean you aren't a leader, you are just different than Commanders, Coaches, and Conductors. You have your own style—be proud of it! But with any style, we must look at what it takes for us to achieve all-around success. And for Counselors, communication is the key.

Here are some examples of poor communication that were printed and distributed in actual church bulletins:

The Fasting and Prayer Conference includes meals.

The sermon this morning is "Jesus walks on the water"
and tonight's sermon will be "Searching for Jesus."

Ladies, don't forget the rummage sale. It's a chance to get rid
of those things not worth keeping around the house. Bring your husbands.

The peacemaking meeting scheduled for today
has been canceled due to a conflict.[1]

Learning how to communicate to each of the different styles will help you feel a bit more comfortable with challenging situations, so I (Lorraine) am providing some case studies for you to review. Take your time with them and see how you might respond in a way that strengthens your leadership, builds your team, and moves you further ahead!

Case Study #1: He Said/She Said

You own a small business where everyone works very closely together. One day, you overhear a heated discussion between two team members. They actually begin to yell at each other, and you feel compelled to step in. You ask Employee A what is going on. Employee A states that she asked Employee B to provide numbers to her by the end of the week so that she could complete a project due by the end of the month.

Before she can finish, Employee B steps in and shouts, "Noooo, you said that two weeks would be fine. I specifically remember telling you that two weeks worked for me and that I would get the numbers to you then."

So upset she is turning red, Employee A burst into tears and says, "You are lying! You just dropped the ball and don't want to get into trouble. Now I won't be able to deliver my project on time, and it is all your fault!"

Before it gets any worse, you must manage the situation and ask them to step into your office. These two employees have seemed to work well together in the past, but they may have some other issues going on.

1. If Employee A is a Coach, how would you talk her through the issues? How would you seek to resolve the issue and conflict?

    _____

    _____

    _____

2. If Employee A is a Counselor, how would you get her to calm down? How would you seek to resolve the issue and conflict?

    _____

    _____

    _____

3. If Employee B is a Conductor, what would work best in getting him to settle down? How would you seek to resolve the issue and conflict?

_____

_____

_____

4. If Employee B is a Commander, how do you approach him without making matters worse? How would you seek to resolve the issue and conflict?

_____

_____

_____

The Heart of the Matter

Because of your Counselor style, you would know these two employees one-on-one and would have some idea of their personal life as well as how they were handling the pressures of work. With Employee A as a Coach, you wouldn't want to embarrass her in front of her co-worker or disregard her feelings. Instead, you would warmly validate her concerns and extend understanding for how frustrated and upset she must be, without taking sides. Simply relating with her should calm her down, but if it doesn't, ask her to take a deep breath. The next step must be to get the truth from her without the emotion. Coaches can often exaggerate and don't naturally focus on details. Use your relational style with a little extra energy to help her explain the exact due date, what is still required, and how important this project is in the big scope of things. To resolve the situation, you must guide her past "he said/she said" and blaming to finding a positive solution.

If Employee A is a Counselor like you, give her a minute to compose herself. Offer her a tissue and something to drink. Don't rush into getting to the bottom of things but rather break it up into smaller questions, allowing her time to respond. If she pulls away and gets quiet, ask her if she needs another minute but continue on with the conversation. Again, you will need to get specifics on the project, not the blow up. Coach her past the disagreement and onto ways to make this work. Be sure to determine how critical this project really is as she may have attached a greater value to it.

Employee B as a Conductor may be very cold at this point because he feels he is not in the wrong. Details *are* his specialty, you know. However, you must not make this a "right/wrong" scenario, but rather one of finding a resolution. You can jump right into questioning what he has done so far, if anything, and how long it would take him to produce the numbers required. Inquire if anyone else on the team could pick up other tasks to enable him to focus his energies on this particular report. Refrain from being too friendly and soft or he may snap back a bit. If you keep it "strictly business," he will shift gears immediately to the end goal.

And finally, if Employee B is a Commander, do not take anything said personally. On the flip side, do not permit the temper tantrum to continue. That stopped when you asked them both into your office. You are in charge. Be direct but not in his face. Get to the bottom line of what exactly he can provide and when. Petition him for a solution and create a challenge within it to motivate him to tackle the project instead of Employee A!

> *"I don't measure a man's success by how high he climbs but by how high he bounces when he hits bottom."*
>
> –George S. Patton[2]

Case Study #2: You Don't Say

You have been asked to participate in a business job placement expo. Candidates are seeking employment in leadership positions. You have twenty minutes to share about your company and why it would be an excellent place to work. In the audience, you have Commanders, Coaches, Counselors, and Conductors.

1. How do you capture and retain the Commanders' attention? What will they be looking for in your company?

   _____

   _____

   _____

2. How do you interact with the Coaches and keep them engaged? What do they want to know about your company?

_____

_____

_____

3. How do you relate with the Counselors and ensure they feel connected with you? What matters most to them about your company?

_____

_____

_____

4. How do you get the Conductors to listen and stay with you? What questions must you answer for them about your company?

_____

_____

_____

Present with Style

Any time you have a group of people, you will have different styles represented. You must speak to each style in order to win them all over. Simply put, if you make your presentation direct, inspiring, supportive, and detailed, you will meet everyone's needs and will not leave anyone behind.

Commanders are going to want to know what your company can do for them. What positions are available, what objectives or goals does the company have, and what challenges need to be overcome? They love a good challenge! You can be very direct and to the point for them when sharing these specifics.

Coaches will be more concerned with the company's mission statement, the way it develops the team, and the company culture. In a nutshell, share with them some stories of how much fun it can be to work at your company. They are interested in the people side of things. Don't be afraid to be more animated during this part of your presentation—and Coaches love jokes!

Counselors will certainly care about your mission statement, but they will also want to hear more about your values. What is most important to the company, and what type of work environment do you have? Be honest about your company and how it treats its people. Share from your heart, which you do very well.

Conductors want the hard, cold facts about the business. How is the company doing, what is your growth projection, and what are your pay ranges? You cannot possibly address every question they have, so come prepared with literature to hand out to them so they can review it at their leisure. Make sure your information is accurate and correct.

If you weave a little bit of each of these into any presentation, you will reach everyone. I know that this matters to you.

Real Life

Real life has many other variables to consider, of course, but you of all types understand that people's experience of the challenges at hand can impact their success. Rather than avoiding the issues, concentrate on helping others, which is your gift.

> *"There is no more noble occupation in the world
> than to assist another human being—to help someone succeed."*
>
> —Alan Loy McGinnis[3]

CHAPTER SIX:
Conductors Know What Works

In Cchapter two, you read some alarming statistics about how very important it is to lead well and build strong relationships with your team. It is paramount to your long-term success. As a Conductor, you are the master of tasks, but you may not always know what is the "right" thing to do with people because tasks are more concrete and people are ever changing (more like mush!). The good news is that you are learning more and more about how to identify the different styles and what will work for them. Your next step is to now apply it.

I know you appreciate working through things, so I (Lorraine) am providing you a couple of case studies that will allow you to think, digest, and then determine what would be the best approach for the particular situation. You have a natural ability toward correctness, so use it and combine it with your newfound knowledge of the leadership styles.

Case Study #1: Show Your Appreciation

You are the newly appointed director of food services for a mid-size hospital. Your leadership team consists of a certified dietician, head cook, a registered nurse, and the janitorial supervisor. During your on-boarding process, you learn that everyone is on the brink of quitting. The last director was a tyrant, so you are told. No one feels appreciated for all the hard work they do or the stress they endure. Your first objective is to turn things around and retain the leadership team because they have extensive background, experience, and knowledge of the hospital. Besides, they all seem to be doing an outstanding job.

1. Your dietician is a Commander. What do you think she values most (time off, bonuses, etc.) and what can you do immediately to show her appreciation?

_____

_____

_____

2. Your cook is a Coach. What do you think he values most, and what can you do immediately to show him appreciation?

_____

_____

_____

3. Your RN is a Counselor. What do you think he values most, and what can you do immediately to show him appreciation?

_____

_____

_____

4. Your janitorial supervisor is a Conductor, like you. What do you think she values most, and what can you do immediately to show her appreciation?

_____

_____

_____

Different Strokes for Different Folks

As leaders, we must understand our people and what motivates them. Everyone is different. Although we have varying backgrounds, using the leadership style model, you can meet needs based upon their primary mode of operation. For instance, your dietician is a goal-oriented individual. You would want to check when her last raise was as money is often a big motivator for Commanders. If she is underpaid, give her the raise. Her tension will decrease because she will feel respected. If her pay is in an appropriate range, you could provide a gift certificate and then set a performance-based bonus plan for the future. This gives her something to strive for and to focus her energies on. You'll find it easy to stick to business with her. Be careful not to get stuck in the details, though, and keep your pace moving along.

Your cook could probably use some cheerleading from you, which isn't the first place you go, but you can do it. Coaches seek approval and praise. He's probably sick of being around hot food and constant time pressures. Something to consider would be a lunch out with him alone. You haven't observed his work personally, but you can share your gratitude for keeping things going smoothly, doing well on performance issues, etc. Do some homework on his department to feel adequately prepared. Sing all the praises you can as he enjoys recognition. Be sure to give him sincere compliments in the presence of others when you can.

Your RN is probably exhausted and hasn't told a soul. Counselors will take a lot, but can finally snap without warning. To head this off at the pass, sit down with him and simply ask how he is doing. He may not immediately answer, or he might feel uncomfortable, so ask what he needs. Does he need a vacation? Does he need more personnel? How is he doing with resources? Then listen. Allow him time to tell how he is doing and to talk with you. Be patient and kind. Consider the person not the task, and you will win him over. Continued support can be provided to him with thank-you cards. These go a very long way, so don't underestimate their power.

Your janitorial supervisor will be the easiest team member to meet with because she is a Conductor like you. You can ask questions about specific job duties and how they are going, knowing that you will receive "just the facts." You would probably give your janitor advance notice to come to the meeting prepared with issues that you could help her with. Working through these together would energize her—and you! Look at ways to improve systems, schedules, etc. She will enjoy it and feel appreciated when you accept her plans.

"The basic cause of most inharmonious human relationships is the tendency to impose our values on other people."

–Robert Anthony[1]

Case Study #2: Let's Work Together

You have volunteered to help bring a satellite-training program to your church. You have been deemed team leader and will be responsible for scheduling meetings with four individuals who are all volunteers as well. You will be in charge of ensuring that their respective areas are on target for the event date, which is in three months. Everyone has received their directives and has lay staff working under them.

1. Your fund raiser is constantly late for all the meetings, arriving in a whirl of activity. She is high energy and apologizes for always being late. She smiles as she shares her great story as to why she was late. What is her dominant style? How can you best communicate with her? How can you keep her on track?

_____

_____

_____

2. Your marketing and PR person attends meetings but does not give you his full attention. He is either receiving telephone calls or making them during the meetings. He indicates to keep pressing on because he has limited time. He often has to leave early. What is his dominant style? How can you best communicate with him? How can you keep him on track?

_____

_____

_____

3. Your facilities guy arrives early, greets you, and then sits down without saying much. He is neat and very organized, bringing his planner to every meeting. He takes incredible notes. What is his dominant style? How can you best communicate with him? How can you keep him on track?

_____

_____

_____

4. Your event planner who will handle the meals and decorations is a sweet gal. She has a warm smile and has compliments for everyone in the room. She is the one who asks if anyone needs anything before the meeting begins. What is her dominant style? How can you best communicate with her? How can you keep her on track?

_____

_____

_____

Doing What Is Right

First of all, no matter who we are, we need to acknowledge that everyone else is not like us. As Conductors, you may struggle with the different styles a bit more, especially the Coaches and Commanders. They can appear improper or brash compared to your measures. However, your team—your life—requires *everyone* to bring balance. Without all the styles, the world would be a scary place. So, relax a bit and extend grace. Your fund raiser, although she isn't prompt, has the gift of gab. As a Coach, she is the perfect person for getting out into the community and building excitement about the event. In addition, she is probably well connected and will get those donations you need so that you can stay within budget. Don't sweat the small stuff and concentrate on keeping the energy positive and providing her places to use her gift. Bring a list of potential vendors and donors so that she can do her magic. Do set a time that she must have everything in to you, and follow up. Don't wait for her to get back to you.

Your marketing and PR man is a mover and shaker. Even though Commanders can come across as rude and annoying, try not to set too many rules on them. Focus on the end results, which is what he will be doing. However, agreeing to dedicate a certain amount of the meeting to go over details uninterrupted is essential. Create an agenda for every meeting and email it in advance so that everyone can be prepared. Put this guy up first so he can report and leave if he has to. As long as he has his marching orders, he will get it done. He's goal oriented and wants to succeed.

Your facilities guy will be right there with you as he is a Conductor too. He most likely will turn in a grid he created with all his duties, team assignments, required resources, and due dates. Each meeting, he will update you with specific details on how the room setup is going, on the progress of the lighting and sound crew, etc. Just as you can get stuck in analyzing and processing, be sure he is moving through to action. If something needs to be researched, set a deadline for it and then make a decision. As the leader, you need to keep this moving along.

Finally, your event planner has a heart of gold and is ideal for addressing all the little things that make an event memorable and enjoyable. As a Counselor, she will be thinking of others, so look out for her. Watch for signs of stress, which are withdrawing, retreating, not responding, etc. Each meeting, ask her how *she* is doing so that you keep your connection strong. If anything for the event changes, let her know immediately and help her understand why so she can change her course smoothly. Try not to dump any last-minute changes on her if you can avoid it.

Real Life

As you well know, there are more details to consider than could ever be covered here, but the bottom line is that by knowing and addressing the specific needs of each person's style, you can help lead them to success. Rather than processing just the details and tasks, you can involve the people, increasing your chances of getting the job done right the first time.

> *"The way we communicate with others and with ourselves*
> *ultimately determines the quality of our lives."*
>
> –Anthony Robbins[2]

CHAPTER SEVEN
Total Quality Leadership

By this point, after reading the book and working through this workbook, you have substantially increased your leadership capacity. Remember our definition: Leadership is influence in the context of positive and proactive relationships. So by now, our hope is that you:

- Know your own leadership style

- Know the leadership style of your primary team members

- Have thought about and practiced effective communication, challenged your team members to leverage their own leadership styles, and experienced conflict resolution with the various leadership styles represented on your team

- Have grown to appreciate the gifts that the various styles bring to the party

All Together Now

In the following exercises, I want to help you to bring it all together so that you can practice Total Quality Leadership. We'll identify your core strengths once again, think about how you can best influence others in the context of positive and proactive relationships, and determine how you can shore up your weaknesses.

1. Which leadership style best represents you? Are you a Commander, Coach, Counselor, or Conductor? Remember, most people have a primary style and a secondary style. Which is your *primary* style and which is your *secondary* style?

_____

_____

_____

2. When people "love" working with you, what aspects of your leadership style are most often talked about? When people "hate" working with you, what aspects of your leadership style are most often talked about?

    _____

    _____

    _____

3. What are the primary and secondary leadership styles of your team members? List their names and both their primary and secondary leadership styles here:

TEAM MEMBER NAME	PRIMARY LEADERSHIP STYLE	SECOND LEADERSHIP STYLE

4. When your team is operating at the very best (positively and proactively), how would you describe the environment and relationships between the team members?

    _____

    _____

    _____

As you operate out of your core philosophy that positive and proactive relationships are the way to influence people toward their highest and greatest personal fulfillment and simultaneously maximize their contributions to the organization, you are well on your way to Total Quality Leadership! This all may seem like a bit of a balancing act—if you are thinking that, you are in good company! I (John) have been in leadership roles for thirty-five years now, and I don't think I've ever gotten it completely right. Leading an organization can be a little bit like directing a musical production that always feels like it is at dress rehearsal stage.

Jan Carzon of the Scandinavian Air System went so far as to say: "All business is show business." We agree. All business is show business. All leadership is show business. All management is show business. That doesn't mean tap dancing; it means shaping your team's values and inspiring action, as a powerful play might affect an audience. It is the opposite of administration and especially, "professional management."[1]

What you "produce" in leadership is the outgrowth of the relationships you build between team members and the way that action is translated from the symbols and focus you create.

5. Clarity in leadership is essential. What are the key values that you want to shape in your teams and organization? If you are successful in shaping those key values, what will be the resulting actions?

_____

_____

_____

Part of the putting it all together is to recognize that, at heart, leveraging your leadership style is all about managing your own leadership with regard to your relationships with others. In their book *The Service Profit Chain*, James Heskett, W. Earl Sasser, and Leonard Schlesinger make the case that no matter what your business, the only way to generate enduring profits is to begin by building the kind of work environment that attracts, focuses, and keeps talented employees.[2] We agree with their focus on personal development and in recognizing that the leadership role is all about "calling forth" the gifts, strengths, and potential of those you work with.

Effective leaders recognize the opportunity they have to call forth the gifts and talents of others. Throughout *Leveraging Your Leadership Style*, we have encouraged you to recognize the strengths not only in your style, but in the styles of others. Alan Nelson, a friend and colleague of mine (John), is the current editor of *Rev! Magazine*. I agree with Alan when he says, "Leadership is a social relationship in which people allow individuals to influence them toward intentional change. Leadership involves more than leaders and what they do. Power ultimately resides in the followers or collaborators."[3] Leaders who are leveraging their leadership style will be working on the strengths of their leadership in partnership with their team members.

6. In what ways have you solicited and received help from your team members? Think of someone on your team who has a different leadership style from yours. How have you come to appreciate his or her unique perspectives and strengths?

    _____

    _____

    _____

7. Consider the make-up of your current team. How are your team members strong in the areas where you are weak? What specific ways does this benefit you? List the areas of their strengths and how they are most complementary to your weaknesses.

    _____

    _____

    _____

Evaluating Ourselves

Recently, our organization has been undergoing substantial transition with several members being moved out of our current team. During this period of time, I (John) have been looking at my own strengths and weaknesses and have been talking with team members about what makes our team healthy and what areas continue to need work. In that process, I've gone back to what I consider the key elements of Total Quality Leadership. I thought it might be helpful to consider those here.

1. Leaders **cast vision.** How can you elevate your team to consider what great future might be theirs if you accomplish your vision?

    _____

    _____

    _____

2. Leaders **create environments**. How can you create contexts where your team can experience health and growth at personal and corporate levels?

_____

_____

_____

3. Leaders **develop systems**. What procedures and processes could you use to ensure consistency and stability in your organization?

_____

_____

_____

4. Leaders **equip other leaders**. How can you help your team members reproduce the health that they are experiencing on your team?

_____

_____

_____

I believe in your ability to grow and develop your team! Part of what you do as a leader is to inspire your team to greatness. Regardless of your leadership style, you have the ability to lift your team to higher heights than have been previously experienced. Your Total Quality Leadership *will* make the difference. Go for greatness!

It's said that Abraham Lincoln often slipped out of the White House on Wednesday evenings to listen to the sermons of Dr. Finnes Gurley at New York Avenue Presbyterian Church. He generally preferred to come and go unnoticed. So when Dr. Gurley knew the President was coming, he left his study door open. On one of those occasions, the President slipped through a side door in the church and took a seat in the minister's study, located just to the side of the sanctuary. There he propped the door open, just wide enough to hear Dr. Gurley. During the walk home, an aide asked Mr. Lincoln his appraisal of the sermon. The President thoughtfully replied, "The content was excellent; he delivered with elegance; he obviously put work into the message." "Then you thought it was an excellent sermon?' questioned the aide. "No" Lincoln answered. "But you said that the content was excellent. It was delivered with eloquence, and it showed how hard he worked," the aide pressed. "That's true," Lincoln said, "But Dr. Gurley forgot the most important ingredient. He forgot to ask us to do something great."

—Unknown[4]

CHAPTER EIGHT
Leadership Quotient

W e have been curious and intrigued about a person's Intelligence Quotient (IQ) since the German psychologist William Stern first coined the phrase in 1912.[1] IQ has typically been used by social sciences as an attempt to measure one's intelligence. Almost as old but not as well known is the Emotional Quotient (EQ) used to "describe an ability, capacity, or skill to perceive, assess, and manage the emotions of one's self, of others, and of groups."[2] Perhaps because I (Lorraine) am not a genius, I haven't given much weight to the IQ measurement when it comes to finding and hiring talent. When I think of high IQ, I envision a brilliant but absent-minded professor like "Doc" Brown in the movie, *Back to the Future*! If you are a high IQ person, please don't take offense. I'm just jealous!

The EQ has certainly caught my attention, though, not as the end-all-be-all determining factor but as yet another area to explore when looking for the right people for the right seats on the right bus (thinking about the metaphor Jim Collins uses in *Good to Great*). EQ assesses areas like maturity, social interface, emotions, self-awareness, empathy, etc. In my opinion, IQ is how our mind works and EQ is how we interact in the world or apply what we know.

Judy Fox Brandt, consultant for Fox & Company, states that IQ or internal processes account for roughly 25 percent of a person's success and basically gets you through school. EQ or behavior, on the other hand, gets you through life and represents about 66 percent of your success. Whew. I'm grateful for that! And, EQ can be improved, but your IQ remains relatively the same through the course of your life. I believe our Leadership Quotient (LQ) is similar. We can grow into tremendous leaders, even if we didn't start that way.

Leadership Intelligence

LQ is what we have been talking about in *Leveraging Your Leadership Style*. It is the ability to adapt one's self to others, which requires being self-*and* others-aware. LQ is what sets us apart from mediocre, average, and trend-following leaders. LQ is leading like Jesus, truly striving for a balanced and appropriate approach to every interaction.

The more you understand yourself and others and then apply that understanding to each situation, the more you are increasing your LQ. The case studies you worked through in this book are perfect examples of beefing up those muscles. The body is an amazing thing. It is designed with everything we need, yet, unless we tap into it, take care of it, and challenge it, it will never reach its full potential. Remember John and I stating early on that we believe God has given each of us the ability to lead? Some people have really worked to develop this ability while others may not have, thus we have some dynamic, powerful leaders and others that are not yet fully developed. The good news is that, just like physical fitness, it is never too late to improve! We can change our bodies by exercising and eating right, and we can become phenomenal leaders, just as God intended, by working on our LQ.

Put It to the Test

As I (Lorraine) said, the best way to get better is to practice. This has been an interactive book, so let's explore some areas of your LQ and see how you are doing.

1. **When confronted with a conflict, do you**

   A. Get excited and ready to fight?

   B. Strategically plan how you will win at any cost?

   C. Run in the other direction?

   D. Seek to understand what the underlying issue is and how to resolve the conflict in a manner that will support all parties?

2. **As you interact with others, do you**

   A. Expect them to read your mind?

   B. Try to adapt your communication and leadership style to better work for them?

   C. Demand that they cater to you?

   D. Passively go with the flow?

3. **When delegating to others, do you**

   A. Focus on the end result, allowing each individual to accomplish the task as he or she sees fit?

   B. Tell them exactly how it needs to be done?

   C. You don't delegate! You do it yourself because no one can be trusted.

   D. Hope that things will go well but don't check in?

4. **When you have to deliver unpleasant news to the troops, do you**

   A. Gather everyone together and communicate in a manner that reaches all parties, being as honest as you can?

   B. Stick your head in the sand and wait until it blows over?

   C. Send an email with the details rather than see everyone face to face?

   D. Tell one person and ask them to forward along the message for you?

5. **When you are given praise from the top on a project which required the efforts of your entire team, do you**

   A. Take all the credit?

   B. Defer all the credit to your team?

C. Say you don't deserve the praise?

D. Graciously accept the praise for you and your team because it was everyone who made it possible?

Take it to the Next Level

The answers to these questions may seem obvious—or they may not. We are all at different stages of our leadership journey, and we all have room to grow. I hope that these at least made you start thinking about your LQ.

For the first question, any time we seek to understand first, we are pausing long enough to evaluate what is really happening. When we do that, we will respond much more appropriately. This is effective in personal relationships too.

For the second question, we may feel that others should be speaking our language since we are in the position of leadership, but the reality is that great leaders think of others. We shouldn't make the focus "us", instead, it should be about influencing, empowering, engaging, motivating, and inspiring others.

For the third question, sometimes we find it easier to just tell people what to do and how do it, but that doesn't take us to the next level of leadership. When we can allow people to be individuals and focus on the end results, then we are leading instead of "managing." True delegation gives the person the chance to be creative with *how* they accomplish the task that has been clearly defined.

For the fourth question, just remember that if you don't clearly and directly communicate what is going on, people will make up their own story. And trust me, what their imaginations create will be way worse than the truth because we have all watched too much television! Seriously, you never go wrong with shooting straight with people. Combine honesty with your ability to adapt to the different styles, and you will have enhanced relationships due to improved communication.

For the last question, don't let your ego get in the way. We all have it; in fact, in order to be successful, you better be using it. But, it has its place. When it comes to praise and compliments for a job well done, don't forget that you are the quarterback. You are only as good as the players on your team.

"No program is possible without change. To achieve the Total Quality Life, you must surrender what you are for what you will become."

–Stan Toler[3]

CONCLUSION
Maximize Your Influence

You are a leader! You are exercising influence in your life on a regular basis as you are engaged in positive and proactive relationships. Because you have taken the time to think through your leadership style and the leadership style of your team members, you are well on your way to leveraging *your* leadership style! Your team members will be thankful for your initiative to enhance your leadership and for your appreciation of their leadership styles. You've invested in your team and helped them develop their self-understanding and skills. You've leveraged your total team capacity.

I (John) played tennis in high school and have played periodically since then. In the middle of the tennis racket is what we call the "sweet spot" where we can maximize our effectiveness with efficiency. That sweet spot is where the greatest impact is made with the least effort. Once you are authentically living out the principles in the *Leveraging Your Leadership Style* book and workbook, you and your team will operate in the "sweet spot" of effectiveness. I'm trusting that the "sweet spot" of your leadership will be a place of fantastic fulfillment. In my own personal experience, when I am operating in the "sweet spot" of my life and leadership, I feel fulfilled even when I am tired—and you will too.

Your capacity for leadership is directly proportional to your ability and willingness to understand and expand the capacities of others and to develop your team together. My prayer and hope has been that you will enjoy the journey of being a leader, and that it will become far more natural to you than ever before. Soon, leadership will "flow" from you organically rather than mechanically through your position or the power of your role.

Truthfully, you are on a leadership journey right now. You read the book and now you have completed the workbook. Whether you are a Commander, a Coach, a Counselor, or a Conductor, you are taking a "road trip" of sorts. You have gone many miles and have learned who is in the car with you! Our prayer for your journey has been that you understand your strengths and your teammates' strengths, and that you desire to help them better leverage their individual strengths. I bet you'll never look at a road trip quite the same way! We are even trusting that your family road trip vacations will take on a new meaning, and be even more enjoyable than before!

Leveraging your leadership style is about becoming all that you were meant to be and coaching others to do the same. I hope we've been able to assist you in the journey. Know that the results that come from your leadership efforts will always be leveraged when you are positive and proactive in the context of relationships that work!

–Dr. John Jackson

Like John, I am an avid tennis fan. As I am finishing up this workbook, the World Team Tennis championship is being televised. As I was watching the other day, I noticed how fun the environment of WTT is compared to the sterile, stoic one at Wimbledon. People actually cheer and scream. They even play music when a superb point is made! One of the big differences I saw was that the players were smiling and enjoying the process a bit more and taking themselves a little less seriously. Yet they were still giving 100 percent and playing to win, and since WTT is about the team, everyone was playing together toward a common goal.

I personally love playing singles, but as I have gotten older, I am not out to destroy my opponent but rather to give my best. My focus is more on my contribution and not just the victory. I'm a more mature player now, concentrating on strategy and execution rather than sheer willpower and speed. And, people matter. In my youth, the other side of the court was "the enemy." Today, I want the other player to have a good experience and to be able to play his or her best. Although I'm not a WTT star, this changed mindset is helping me settle into a more satisfying tennis career of my own.

As you get in a groove with your leadership style, my hope for you is that you play the game for the benefit of all involved, and actually enjoy the journey of life and leadership. With more tools on your belt, coupled with a greater awareness of others, you should be feeling better equipped to lead no matter where you are and what your title or role. This doesn't mean that life won't throw you some curve balls, but you will have more skill and heart to face them. Yes, heart. Throughout our time together, I hope you have come to appreciate the importance of caring for those you lead. I know it comes easier for those who are Coaches and Counselors. However, if we are truly going to be better leaders than some of the recent examples in the media, we must care. Trust me, Commanders and Conductors, you will receive major blessings for your efforts—here on earth and in Heaven! We have to take our leadership the extra step and let those we lead know how much we care. Understanding and applying the leadership styles is a perfect way to do that.

This workbook gave you some things to think about, process, and consider. Any time we take a new skill or knowledge and practice applying it to such things as the case studies in chapters three through six, we have dramatically increased our chances of assimilating it into our daily practice. Now start using it in life. In every situation you practice adapting yourself to others, you will become stronger and better. The exciting part is that things will start going more smoothly and more easily because you are building bridges, not creating barriers.

Life is too short. Not a single one of us gets out of it alive. The more time we spend enriching others, the more blessed we become. Leadership is an awesome avenue for making a difference in the lives of others and having an influence upon them. That brings us full circle.

I pray that your influence multiplies. As you share what you know with others, we can start to create a more harmonious, empowering, respectful, loving, and productive world. We'll have you to thank! Blessings.

–**Lorraine Bossé-Smith**

Workbook Notes

Chapter One: Building Bridges

1. Marcus Buckingham, *First Break All the Rules* (New York: Simon & Schuster, 1999), 85.

Chapter Two: Create Stronger Relationships

1. Jay J. Jamrog, "The Perfect Storm," *AMA Business Brief* (American Management Association, adapted from *The Perfect Storm: The Future of Retention and Engagement* by Jay Jamrog© 2004, Human Resources Institute, St. Perersburg, Florida), 3.

2. Ibid.

3. John Maxwell,. *The Influential Leader*, Live Simulcast, Cornerstone Community Church; Wildomar, CA, April 2004.

4. Jamrog, "The Perfect Storm," *AMA Business Brief,* 3.

5. Judith Glaser, "The New Leader: Go From Dictating to Developing," *Leadership Excellence* 24, no. 4 (Executive Excellence Publishing, Seymour, CT), April 2007, 8.

6. Maxwell, *The Influential Leader*, Live Simulcast.

7. Ibid.

8. Robert Townsend quoted in Glenn Van Ekeren, *The Speaker's Sourcebook II* (Englewood Cliffs, NJ: Prentice Hall), 223.

9. Jamrog, "The Perfect Storm," *AMA Business Brief,* 3.

10. Ibid, 7.

11. Thomas J. Peters and Nancy Austin quoted in Van Ekeren, *The Speaker's Sourcebook II*, 318.

Chapter Three: Commanders Get'er Done!

1. Carl Jung quoted in Van Ekeren, *The Speaker's Sourcebook II*, 361.

Chapter Five: Counselors Know Why It Matters

1. "Actual Announcements from Church Bulletins," Web. 6 April 2007, swapmeetdave.com/Humor/Religious.htm

2. George S. Patton, "Do Not Say: I Have Done Enough." E-letter edited by Ken Keller (Renaissance Executive Forums), 5 July 2007, 1.

3. Alan Loy McGinnis quoted in Van Ekeren, *The Speaker's Sourcebook II*, 122.

Chapter Six: Conductors Know What Works

1. Robert Anthony quoted in Van Ekeren, *The Speaker's Sourcebook II*, 317.

2. Anthony Robbins quoted in Van Ekeren, *The Speaker's Sourcebook II*, 71 .

Chapter Seven: Total Quality Leadership

1. Thomas J. Peters and Nancy Austin, *A Passion for Excellence* (New York: Warner Books, 1985), 311.

2. Marcus Buckingham and Curt Coffman, *First, Break All The Rules* (New York: Simon & Schuster, 1999), 21.

3. Alan Nelson, *Spirituality & Leadership: Harnessing the Wisdom, Guidance, and Power of the Soul* (Colorado Springs, CO: NavPress Publishing Group, 2002), 23.

4. Ken Blanchard and Jesse Stoner, *Full Steam Ahead, Unleash the Power of Vision in Your Company and Your Life* (San Francisco: Berrett-Koehler Publishers, 2003), 6-7.

Chapter Eight: Leadership Quotient

1. "Intelligence Quotient," *Wikipedia*, n.d. web. 23 July 2007, en.wikipedia.org/wiki/intelligence_quotient.

2. "Emotional Intelligence," *Wikipedia*, n.d. web. 23 July 2007, en.wikipedia.org/wiki/emotional_intelligence.

3. Stan Toler, *Total Quality Life: Strategies for Purposeful Living* (Indianapolis: Wesleyan Publishing House, 2007), 115.

Workbook Bibliography

"Actual Announcements from Church Bulletins." Web. 6 April 2007. swapmeetdave.com/ Humor/Religious.htm

Buckingham, Marcus and Curt Coffman. *First, Break All the Rules*. New York: Simon & Schuster, 1999.

Fox-Brandt, Judy. *Emotional Intelligence: What It Is and Why It Matters to Your Business*. Presentation made to Executive Forums, Rancho Cucamonga, CA. 13 June, 2007.

Glaser, Judith. *The New Leader: Go From Dictating to Developing. Article in Leadership Excellence* 24, no. 4. April 2007.

"Emotional Intelligence." *Wikipedia*, n.d. web. 23 July 2007. en.wikipedia.org/wiki/ emotional_intelligence.

"Intelligence Quotient." *Wikipedia*, n.d. web. 23 July 2007. en.wikipedia.org/wiki/ intelligence_quotient.

Jackson, John. *PastorPreneur*. Carson City, NV. VisionQuest Ministries, 2003.

Jamrog, Jay J. *The Perfect Storm: The Future of Retention and Engagement*. St. Petersburg, FL: Human Resource Institute, 2004 (Adapted Version at AMAnet.org).

Kawasaki, Guy. "How to Change The World." Web. n.d. guykawasaki.com/blog/.

Maxwell, John C. *The Influential Leader*. Live Simulcast, Cornerstone Community Church; Wildomar, CA, April 2004.

Nelson, Alan. *Spirituality & Leadership: Harnessing the Wisdom, Guidance, and Power of the Soul*. Colorado Springs, CO: NavPress Publishing Group, 2002.

Patton, George S. "Do Not Say: I Have Done Enough." E-letter edited by Ken Keller, Renaissance Executive Forums, 5 July 2007.

Peters, Thomas J. and Nancy Austin. *A Passion for Excellence*. New York, NY: Warner Books, 1985.

Sanborn, Mark. *The Fred Factor*. New York, NY: Doubleday Books, 2004.

Sanders, Tim. *The Likeability Factor*. New York, NY: Crown, 2005.

Toler, Stan. *Total Quality Life: Strategies for Purposeful Living.* Indianapolis, IN: Wesleyan Publishing House, 2007.

Van Ekeren, Glenn. *The Speaker's Sourcebook II.* Englewood Cliffs, NJ: Prentice Hall, 1994.

About the Authors

Prior to joining William Jessup University as its sixth President in March 2011, John served as the Executive Director of Thriving Churches International and as a senior leader of Bayside Church, Granite Bay, California. He is the Founding Pastor of LifePoint Church in Minden, Nevada, and previously was the Executive Minister of the American Baptist Churches of the Pacific Southwest (now Transformation Ministries) where he was responsible to serve more than 270 churches in four Western states. John also served as the Senior Pastor and in several staff roles at First Baptist Church of Oxnard and as the Youth Pastor at First Baptist Church of Buena Park. Dr. Jackson earned both his Ph.D. and M.A. in Educational Administration and Organizational Studies from the University of California, Santa Barbara; M.A. in Theology (Christian Formation and Discipleship) at Fuller Theological Seminary; and a B.A. in Religion (Christian History and Thought) from Chapman University.

His strong background in executive and organizational leadership has given him the opportunity to come alongside high impact churches and leaders in national and global settings to strengthen their organizational leadership and communication skills. John is committed to leveraging his Kingdom influence through strategic relationships.

Dr. Jackson has written and co-authored six books: *Finding Your Place in God's Plan, God Size Your Church, Leveraging Your Communication Style, Leveraging Your Leadership Style, Pastorpreneur* and *High Impact Church Planting.*

Dr. Jackson is married to Pamela Harrison Jackson and they make their home in Rocklin, CA. They have five children, three of whom are married. They are still waiting for grandchildren.

For information on speaking engagements and seminar resources please visit: DrJohnJackson.com.

Lorraine Bossé-Smith has over 30 years experience in corporate America as a leader and change agent. She has held key positions in a publishing house, a multi-million dollar catalog company, as well as space foundation, overseeing staff and critical company objectives. Since 1996, she has served a variety of clients nationwide through her own business, offering business consulting, corporate training, and executive coaching. As a dynamic speaker, Lorraine delivers incredible insights with actionable information for all.

Lorraine is the author of *I Want My Life Back, Leveraging Your Communication Style, Fit Over 50, Finally FIT,* and *A Healthier, Happier You.* Lorraine is a Certified Professional Behavior Analyst (CPBA) and Certified Professional Motivators Analyst (CPMA), and holds a B.S. in Business Administration with minors in Marketing and Communications. You will often hear her on live radio and television shows. Let her help rewire your business and life for success!

BE FIT TO LEAD
w/other resources by Lorraine

For any woman who wears many hats, manages multiple schedules and wonders how she will fit it all in without losing her mind! This book helps find control and order in chaos.

With encouragement, practical tips and laughs, readers can get their life back!

$ 14.00 each

Discouraged and frustrated because you can't find the right program or stick with it? Readers will take an exclusive assessment to determine their FIT (Fitness Individuality Trait) and then customize a new program to FINALLY reach their health goals.

Perfect for anyone at any age!

$ 14.00 each

This book is for anyone who wants their next chapter of life to be their BEST one!

Readers will uncover myths and learn the truth about the aging process. Then, they will be encouraged and inspired to develop a fitness program for their specific stage of life. It is NEVER too late to get healthy!

$ 15.00 each

(623) 582-1578 * www.lorrainebosse-smith.com

Dr. Jackson has a number of speaking resources available for free review at drjohnjackson.com/resources. In addition, all of his book titles are available on Amazon and other electronic retailers. Titles include:

God Size Your Church

Pastorpreneur

Leveraging Your Communication Style

Finding Your Place in God's Plan

High Impact Church Planting

Dr. Jackson speaks and consults regularly to for-profit and non-profit organizations on topics including leadership, communication, and spiritual growth. If you would like to schedule Dr. Jackson for a speech or for consultation, please email him at jjackson@jessup.edu